The Methuen Modern Plays series has always been at the forefront of modern playwriting. Since 1959, the series has reflected the most exciting developments in modern drama, making the most significant plays widely available in paperback.

Hay Fever

Hay Fever, one of the best-loved of all Noël Coward's plays was reckoned by Tyrone Guthrie to have 'as good a chance of immortality as any work of an author now living' and as Noël Coward himself wrote, '*Hay Fever* is considered by many to be my best comedy' and 'far and away one of the most difficult plays to perform that I have ever encountered. To begin with it has no plot at all, and remarkably little action. Its general effectiveness therefore depends upon expert technique from each and every member of the cast . . . The Press naturally and inevitably described it as "thin", "tenuous" and "trivial" because those are their stock phrases for anything later in date and lighter in texture than *The Way of the World*, and it ran, tenuously and triumphantly for a year.'

Noël Coward was born in 1899 in Teddington, Middlesex. He made his name as a playwright with *The Vortex* (1924), in which he also appeared. His numerous other successful plays included *Fallen Angels* (1925), *Hay Fever* (1925), *Private Lives* (1933), *Design for Living* (1933), and *Blithe Spirit* (1941). During the war he wrote screenplays such as *Brief Encounter* (1944) and *This Happy Breed* (1942). In the fifties he began a new career as a cabaret entertainer. He published volumes of verse and a novel, *Pomp and Circumstance* (1960), two volumes of autobiography and four volumes of short stories: *To Step Aside* (1939), *Star Quality* (1951), *Pretty Polly Barlow* (1964) and *Bon Voyage* (1967). He was knighted in 1970 and died three years later in Jamaica.

Contents

Published by Methuen 2002
Methuen Publishing Ltd
215 Vauxhall Bridge Road,
London SW1V 1EJ

3 5 7 9 10 8 6 4 2

Hay Fever was first published in 1925 by Ernest Benn as Contemporary British
Dramatists Volume 27 and republished by Heinemann in 1934 Play Parade Vol. 2.
This edition was first published in 1983 in paperback as a Methuen Modern Play

Methuen Publishing Limited Reg. No. 3543167

A CIP catalogue record for this book
is available from the British Library

ISBN 0 413 54090 1

Typeset by Deltatype Ltd, Birkenhead, Merseyside
Printed and bound in Great Britain by
Cox & Wyman Ltd, Reading, Berkshire

Caution

Chronology

1899   16 December, Noël Pierce Coward born in
       Teddington, Middlesex, eldest surviving son of
       Arthur Coward, piano salesman and Violet (*née*
       Veitch). A 'brazen, odious little prodigy', his early
       circumstances were of refined suburban poverty.

1907   First public appearances in school and community
       concerts.

1908   Family moved to Battersea and took in lodgers.

1911   First professional appearance as Prince Mussel in *The
       Goldfish*, produced by Lila Field at the Little Theatre,
       and revived in same year at Crystal Palace and
       Royal Court Theatre. Cannard the page-boy, in *The
       Great Name* at the Prince of Wales Theatre, and
       William in *Where the Rainbow Ends* with Charles
       Hawtrey's Company at the Savoy Theatre.

1912   Directed *The Daisy Chain* and stage-managed *The
       Prince's Bride* at Savoy in series of matinées featuring
       the work of the children of the *Rainbow* cast.
       Mushroom in *An Autumn Idyll*, ballet, Savoy.

1913   An angel (Gertrude Lawrence was another) in Basil
       Dean's production of *Hannele*. Slightly in *Peter Pan*,
       Duke of York's.

1914   Toured in *Peter Pan*. Collaborated with fellow
       performer Esmé Wynne on songs, sketches, and
       short stories – 'beastly little whimsies'.

1915   Admitted to sanatorium for tuberculosis.

1916   Five-month tour as Charley in *Charley's Aunt*. Walk-
       on in *The Best of Luck*, Drury Lane. Wrote first full-
       length song, 'Forbidden Fruit'. Basil Pycroft in *The
       Light Blues*, produced by Robert Courtneidge, with
       daughter Cicely also in cast, Shaftesbury. Short spell
       as dancer at Elysée Restaurant (subsequently the
       Café de Paris). Jack Morrison in *The Happy Family*,
       Prince of Wales.

1917   'Boy pushing barrow' in D.W. Griffith's film *Hearts of
       the World*. Co-author with Esmé Wynne of one-acter

Ida Collaborates, Theatre Royal, Aldershot. Ripley Guildford in *The Saving Grace*, with Charles Hawtrey, 'who ... taught me many points of comedy acting', Garrick. Family moved to Pimlico and re-opened boarding house.

1918 Called-up for army. Medical discharge after nine months. Wrote unpublished novels *Cats and Dogs* (loosely based on Shaw's *You Never Can Tell*) and the unfinished *Cherry Pan* ('dealing in a whimsical vein with the adventures of a daughter of Pan'), and lyrics for Darewski and Joel, including 'When You Come Home on Leave' and 'Peter Pan'. Also composed 'Tamarisk Town'. Sold short stories to magazines. Wrote plays *The Rat Trap*, *The Last Trick* (unproduced) and *The Impossible Wife* (unproduced). Courtenay Borner in *Scandal*, Strand. *Woman and Whiskey* (co-author Esmé Wynne) produced at Wimbledon Theatre.

1919 Ralph in *The Knight of the Burning Pestle*, Birmingham Repertory, played with 'a stubborn Mayfair distinction' demonstrating a 'total lack of understanding of the play'. Collaborated on *Crissa*, an opera, with Esmé Wynne and Max Darewski (unproduced). Wrote *I'll Leave It to You*.

1920 Bobbie Dermott in *I'll Leave It to You*, New Theatre. Wrote play *Barriers Down* (unproduced). *I'll Leave It to You* published, London.

1921 On holiday in Alassio, met Gladys Calthrop for the first time. Clay Collins in American farce *Polly with a Past*: during the run 'songs, sketches, and plays were bursting out of me'. Wrote *The Young Idea*, *Sirocco*, and *The Better Half*. First visit to New York, and sold parts of *A Withered Nosegay* to *Vanity Fair* and short-story adaptation of *I'll Leave It to You* to *Metropolitan*. House-guest of Laurette Taylor and Hartley Manners, whose family rows inspired the Bliss household in *Hay Fever*.

1922 *Bottles and Bones* (sketch) produced in benefit for Newspaper Press Fund, Drury Lane. *The Better Half* produced in 'grand guignol' season, Little Theatre. Started work on songs and sketches for *London Calling!* Adapted Louise Verneuil's *Pour avoir Adrienne* (unproduced). Wrote *The Queen Was in the Parlour* and *Mild Oats*.

1923   Sholto Brent in *The Young Idea*, Savoy. Juvenile lead in *London Calling!* Wrote *Weatherwise*, *Fallen Angels*, and *The Vortex*.

1924   Wrote *Hay Fever* (which Marie Tempest at first refused to do, feeling it was 'too light and plotless and generally lacking in action') and *Easy Virtue*. Nicky Lancaster in *The Vortex*, produced at Everyman by Norman MacDermot.

1925   Established as a social and theatrical celebrity. Wrote *On With the Dance* with London opening in spring followed by *Fallen Angels* and *Hay Fever*. *Hay Fever* and *Easy Virtue* produced, New York. Wrote silent screen titles for Gainsborough Films.

1926   Toured USA in *The Vortex*. Wrote *This Was a Man*, refused a licence by Lord Chamberlain but produced in New York (1926), Berlin (1927), and Paris (1928). *Easy Virtue*, *The Queen Was in the Parlour*, and *The Rat Trap* produced, London. Played Lewis Dodd in *The Constant Nymph*, directed by Basil Dean. Wrote *Semi-Monde* and *The Marquise*. Bought Goldenhurst Farm, Kent, as country home. Sailed for Hong Kong on holiday but trip broken in Honolulu by nervous breakdown.

1927   *The Marquise* opened in London while Coward was still in Hawaii, and *The Marquise* and *Fallen Angels* produced, New York. Finished writing *Home Chat*. *Sirocco* revised after discussions with Basil Dean and produced, London.

1928   Clark Storey in Behrman's *The Second Man*, directed by Dean. Gainsborough Films productions of *The Queen Was in the Parlour*, *The Vortex* (starring Ivor Novello), and *Easy Virtue* (directed by Alfred Hitchcock) released – but only the latter, freely adapted, a success. *This Year of Grace!* produced,

London, and with Coward directing and in cast,
New York. Made first recording, featuring numbers
from this show. Wrote *Concerto* for Gainsborough
Films, intended for Ivor Novello, but never
produced. Started writing *Bitter-Sweet*.

1929   Played in *This Year of Grace!* (USA) until spring.
Directed *Bitter-Sweet*, London and New York. Set off
on travelling holiday in Far East.

1930   On travels wrote *Private Lives* (1929) and song 'Mad
Dogs and Englishmen', the latter on the road from
Hanoi to Saigon. In Singapore joined the Quaints,
company of strolling English players, as Stanhope for
three performances of *Journey's End*. On voyage home
wrote *Post-Mortem*, which was 'similar to my
performance as Stanhope: confused, under-rehearsed
and hysterical'. Directed and played Elyot Chase in
Private Lives, London, and Fred in *Some Other Private
Lives*. Started writing *Cavalcade* and unfinished novel
Julian Kane.

1931   Elyot Chase in New York production of *Private Lives*.
Directed *Cavalcade*, London. Film of *Private Lives*
produced by MGM. Set off on trip to South
America.

1932   On travels wrote *Design for Living* (hearing that Alfred
Lunt and Lynn Fontanne finally free to work with
him) and material for new revue including songs
'Mad about the Boy', 'Children of the Ritz' and
'The Party's Over Now'. Produced in London as
Words and Music, with book, music, and lyrics
exclusively by Coward and directed by him. The
short-lived Noël Coward Company, independent
company which enjoyed his support, toured UK with
Private Lives, *Hay Fever*, *Fallen Angels*, and *The Vortex*.

1933   Directed *Design for Living*, New York, and played Leo.
Films of *Cavalcade*, *To-Night Is Ours* (remake of *The
Queen Was in the Parlour*), and *Bitter-Sweet* released.
Directed London revival of *Hay Fever*. Wrote
Conversation Piece as vehicle for Yvonne Printemps,
and hit song 'Mrs Worthington'.

1934   Directed *Conversation Piece* in London and played
       Paul. Cut links with C. B. Cochran and formed own
       management in partnership with John C. Wilson.
       Appointed President of the Actors' Orphanage, in
       which he invested great personal commitment until
       resignation in 1956. Directed Kaufman and Ferber's
       Theatre Royal, Lyric, and Behrman's *Biography*, Globe.
       Film of *Design for Living* released, London. *Conversation
       Piece* opened, New York. Started writing
       autobiography, *Present Indicative*. Wrote *Point Valaine*.

1935   Directed *Point Valaine*, New York. Played lead in film
       The Scoundrel (Astoria Studios, New York). Wrote *To-
       Night at 8.30*.

1936   Directed and played in *To-Night at 8.30*, London and
       New York. Directed *Mademoiselle* by Jacques Deval,
       Wyndham's.

1937   Played in *To-Night at 8.30*, New York, until second
       breakdown in health in March. Directed (and
       subsequently disowned) Gerald Savory's *George and
       Margaret*, New York. Wrote *Operette*, with hit song
       'The Stately Homes of England'. *Present Indicative*
       published, London and New York.

1938   Directed *Operette*, London. *Words and Music* revised for
       American production as *Set to Music*. Appointed
       adviser to newly formed Royal Naval Film
       Corporation.

1939   Directed New York production of *Set to Music*.
       Visited Soviet Union and Scandinavia. Wrote *Present
       Laughter* and *This Happy Breed*: rehearsals stopped by
       declaration of war. Wrote for revue *All Clear*,
       London. Appointed to head Bureau of Propaganda
       in Paris, to liaise with French Ministry of
       Information, headed by Jean Giraudoux and André
       Maurois. This posting prompted speculative attacks
       in the press, prevented by wartime secrecy from
       getting a clear statement of the exact nature of his
       work (in fact unexceptional and routine). Troop
       concert in Arras with Maurice Chevalier. *To Step
       Aside* (short story collection) published.

1940   Increasingly 'oppressed and irritated by the Paris routine'. Visits USA to report on American isolationism and attitudes to war in Europe. Return to Paris prevented by German invasion. Returned to USA to do propaganda work for Ministry of Information. Propaganda tour of Australia and New Zealand, and fund-raising for war charities. Wrote play *Time Remembered* (unproduced).

1941   Mounting press attacks in England because of time spent allegedly avoiding danger and discomfort of Home Front. Wrote *Blithe Spirit*, produced in London (with Coward directing) and New York. MGM film of *Bitter-Sweet* (which Coward found 'vulgar' and 'lacking in taste') released, London. Wrote screenplay for *In Which We Serve*, based on the sinking of HMS *Kelly*. Wrote songs including 'London Pride', 'Could You Please Oblige Us with a Bren Gun?', and 'Imagine the Duchess's Feelings'.

1942   Produced and co-directed (with David Lean) *In Which We Serve*, and appeared as Captain Kinross (Coward considered the film 'an accurate and sincere tribute to the Royal Navy'). Played in countrywide tour of *Blithe Spirit*, *Present Laughter*, and *This Happy Breed*, and gave hospital and factory concerts. MGM film of *We Were Dancing* released.

1943   Played Garry Essendine in London production of *Present Laughter* and Frank Gibbons in *This Happy Breed*. Produced *This Happy Breed* for Two Cities Films. Wrote 'Don't Let's Be Beastly to the Germans', first sung on BBC Radio (then banned on grounds of lines 'that Goebbels might twist'). Four-month tour of Middle East to entertain troops.

1944   February–September, toured South Africa, Burma, India, and Ceylon. Troop concerts in France and 'Stage Door Canteen Concert' in London. Screenplay of *Still Life*, as *Brief Encounter*. *Middle East Diary*, an account of his 1943 tour, published, London and New York – where a reference to 'mournful little boys from Brooklyn' inspired

formation of a lobby for the 'Prevention of Noël Coward Re-entering America'.

1945   *Sigh No More*, with hit song 'Matelot', completed and produced, London. Started work on *Pacific 1860*. Film of *Brief Encounter* released.

1946   Started writing '*Peace in Our Time*'. Directed *Pacific 1860*, London.

1947   Gary Essendine in London revival of *Present Laughter*. Supervised production of '*Peace in Our Time*'. *Point Valaine* produced, London. Directed American revival of *To-Night at 8.30*. Wrote *Long Island Sound* (unproduced).

1948   Replaced Graham Payn briefly in American tour of *To-Night at 8.30*, his last stage appearance with Gertrude Lawrence. Wrote screenplay for Gainsborough film of *The Astonished Heart*. Max Aramont in *Joyeux Chagrins* (French production of *Present Laughter*). Built house at Blue Harbour, Jamaica.

1949   Christian Faber in film of *The Astonished Heart*. Wrote *Ace of Clubs* and *Home and Colonial* (produced as *Island Fling* in USA and *South Sea Bubble* in UK).

1950   Directed *Ace of Clubs*, London. Wrote *Star Quality* (short stories) and *Relative Values*.

1951   Deaths of Ivor Novello and C. B. Cochran. Paintings included in charity exhibition in London. Wrote *Quadrille*. One-night concert at Theatre Royal, Brighton, followed by season at Café de Paris, London, and beginning of new career as leading cabaret entertainer. Directed *Relative Values*, London, which restored his reputation as a playwright after run of post-war flops. *Island Fling* produced, USA.

1952   Charity cabaret with Mary Martin at Café de Paris for Actors' Orphanage. June cabaret season at Café de Paris. Directed *Quadrille*, London. '*Red Peppers*', *Fumed Oak*, and *Ways and Means* (from *To-Night at 8.30*) filmed as *Meet Me To-Night*. September, death of Gertrude Lawrence: 'no one I have ever known, however brilliant . . . has contributed quite what she

contributed to my work'.

1953 Completed second volume of autobiography, *Future Indefinite*. King Magnus in Shaw's *The Apple Cart*. Cabaret at Café de Paris, again 'a triumphant success'. Wrote *After the Ball*.

1954 *After the Ball* produced, UK. July, mother died. September, cabaret season at Café de Paris. November, Royal Command Performance, London Palladium. Wrote *Nude With Violin*.

1955 June, opened in cabaret for season at Desert Inn, Las Vegas, and enjoyed 'one of the most sensational successes of my career'. Played Hesketh-Baggott in film of *Around the World in Eighty Days*, for which he wrote own dialogue. October, directed and appeared with Mary Martin in TV spectacular *Together with Music* for CBS, New York. Revised *South Sea Bubble*.

1956 Charles Condomine in television production of *Blithe Spirit*, for CBS, Hollywood. For tax reasons took up Bermuda residency. Resigned from presidency of the Actors' Orphanage. *South Sea Bubble* produced, London. Directed and played part of Frank Gibbons in television production of *This Happy Breed* for CBS, New York. Co-directed *Nude With Violin* with John Gielgud (Eire and UK), opening to press attacks on Coward's decision to live abroad. Wrote play *Volcano* (unproduced).

1957 Directed and played Sebastien in *Nude With Violin*, New York. *Nude With Violin* published, London.

1958 Played Gary Essendine in *Present Laughter* alternating with *Nude With Violin* on US West Coast tour. Wrote ballet *London Morning* for London Festival Ballet. Wrote *Look After Lulu!*

1959 *Look After Lulu!* produced, New York, and by English Stage Company at Royal Court, London. Film roles of Hawthorne in *Our Man in Havana* and ex-King of Anatolia in *Surprise Package*. *London Morning* produced by London Festival Ballet. Sold home in Bermuda and took up Swiss residency. Wrote *Waiting in the Wings*.

1960 *Waiting in the Wings* produced, Eire and UK. *Pomp and*

Circumstance (novel) published, London and New York.

1961   Alec Harvey in television production of *Brief Encounter* for NBC, USA. Directed American production of *Sail Away*. *Waiting in the Wings* published, New York.

1962   Wrote music and lyrics for *The Girl Who Came to Supper* (adaptation of Rattigan's *The Sleeping Prince*, previously filmed as *The Prince and the Showgirl*). *Sail Away* produced, UK.

1963   *The Girl Who Came to Supper* produced, USA. Revival of *Private Lives* at Hampstead signals renewal of interest in his work.

1964   'Supervised' production of *High Spirits*, musical adaptation of *Blithe Spirit*, Savoy. Introduced Granada TV's 'A Choice of Coward' series, which included *Present Laughter*, *Blithe Spirit*, *The Vortex*, and *Design for Living*. Directed *Hay Fever* for National Theatre, first living playwright to direct his own work there. *Pretty Polly Barlow* (short story collection) published.

1965   Played the landlord in film, *Bunny Lake is Missing*. Wrote *Suite in Three Keys*. Badly weakened by attack of amoebic dysentery contracted in Seychelles.

1966   Played in *Suite in Three Keys*, London, which taxed his health further. Started adapting his short story *Star Quality* for the stage.

1967   Caesar in TV musical version of *Androcles and the Lion* (score by Richard Rodgers), New York. Witch of Capri in film *Broom*, adaptation of Tennessee Williams's play *The Milk Train Doesn't Stop Here Any More*. Lorn Loraine, Coward's manager, and friend for many years, died, London. Worked on new volume of autobiography, *Past Conditional*. *Bon Voyage* (short story collection) published.

1968   Played Mr Bridger, the criminal mastermind, in *The Italian Job*.

1970   Awarded knighthood in New Year's Honours List.

1971   Tony Award, USA, for Distinguished Achievement in the Theatre.

1973   26 March, died peacefully at his home in Blue Harbour, Jamaica. Buried on Firefly Hill.

Hay Fever

Noël Coward

Methuen Drama

Characters

Judith Bliss
David Bliss
Sorel Bliss
Simon Bliss
Myra Arundel
Richard Greatham
Jackie Coryton
Sandy Tyrell
Clara

Act One
Saturday afternoon

Act Two
Saturday evening

Act Three
Sunday morning

The action of the play takes place in the Hall of the **Blisses'** house at Cookham in June.

Act One

Scene   *The Hall of* **David Bliss**'s *house is very comfortable and extremely untidy. There are several of* **Simon**'s *cartoons scattered about the walls, masses of highly-coloured American and classical music strewn about the piano, and comfortable furniture. A staircase ascends to a small balcony leading to the bedrooms,* **David**'s *study and* **Simon**'s *room. There is a door leading to the library down L. A service door above it under the stairs. There are french windows at back and front door on the R.*

When the curtain rises it is about three o'clock on a Saturday afternoon in June.

Simon, *in an extremely dirty tennis shirt and baggy grey flannel trousers, is kneeling in the middle of the floor, drawing on cartridge paper, of which there are two pieces by him.*

Sorel, *more neatly dressed, is stretched on L. end of the sofa, reading a very violently-bound volume of poems which have been sent to her by an aspiring friend.*

Sorel   Listen to this, Simon. (*She reads.*)
  'Love's a Trollop stained with wine,
  Clawing at the breasts of Adolescence,
  Nuzzling, tearing, shrieking, beating—
  God, why were we fashioned so!'
She laughs.

Simon (*looking up from his drawing*)   The poor girl's potty!

Sorel   I wish she hadn't sent me the beastly book. I must say something nice about it.

Simon   The binding's very dashing.

Sorel   She used to be such fun before she married that gloomy little man.

Simon   She was always a fierce poseuse. It's so silly of people to try and cultivate the artistic temperament. *Au fond* she's just a normal, bouncing Englishwoman.

Sorel You didn't shave this morning.

Simon I know I didn't, but I'm going to in a minute, when I've finished this. (*Pointing to drawing.*)

Sorel I sometimes wish *we* were more normal and bouncing, Simon.

Simon Why? (*Starts to draw again.*)

Sorel I should like to be a fresh, open-air girl with a passion for games.

Simon Thank God you're not.

Sorel It would be so soothing.

Simon Not in this house.

Sorel Where's Mother?

Simon In the garden, practising.

Sorel Practising?

Simon (*stops drawing and looks at* **Sorel**) She's learning the names of the flowers by heart.

Sorel What's she up to?

Simon I don't know. (*Looks down at drawing.*) Damn! That's crooked.

Sorel I *always* distrust her when she becomes the Squire's lady.

Simon So do I. (*Starts drawing again.*)

Sorel She's been at it hard all day – she tapped the barometer this morning.

Simon She's probably got a plan about impressing somebody.

Sorel (*taking a cigarette from table behind sofa*) I wonder who.

Simon Some dreary, infatuated young man will appear

soon, I expect.

Sorel   Not to-day? (*Lights cigarette.*) You don't think she's asked anyone down to-day, do you?

Simon (*stops drawing and looks up*)   I don't know. Has Father noticed anything?

Sorel   No; he's too immersed in work.

Simon   Perhaps Clara will know.

Sorel   Yell for her.

Simon (*rises and goes up C., calling off door below stairs*)   Clara! Clara! . . .

Sorel (*moves to R. end of sofa*)   Oh, Simon, I *do* hope she hasn't asked anyone down to-day.

Simon (*coming down to R. end of sofa*)   Why? Have you?

Sorel   Yes.

Simon (*crossly*)   Why on earth didn't you tell me?

Sorel   I didn't think you'd care one way or another.

Simon   Who is it?

Sorel   Richard Greatham.

Simon (*goes back to drawing*)   How exciting! I've never heard of him.

Sorel   I shouldn't flaunt your ignorance if I were you – it makes you look silly.

Simon (*rising and picking up one sheet of cartridge paper and pencil*)   Well, that's done. (*He rolls up the cartridge paper.*)

Sorel   Everybody's heard of Richard Greatham.

Simon (*amiably*)   How lovely for them! (*Going to piano.*)

Sorel   He's a frightfully well-known diplomatist – I met him at the Mainwarings' dance.

Simon   He'll need all his diplomacy here. (*Puts pencil on piano.*)

Sorel   I warned him not to expect good manners, but I hope you'll be as pleasant to him as you can.

Simon (*gently – moves to C.*)   I've never met any diplomatists, Sorel, but as a class I'm extremely prejudiced against them. They're so suave and polished and debonair.

Sorel   You could be a little more polished without losing caste.

Simon (*moves to* **Sorel**)   Will he have the papers with him?

Sorel   What papers?

Simon (*vaguely*)   Oh, any papers. (*Goes up C. and puts paper on chair.*)

Sorel   I wish you'd confine your biting irony to your caricatures, Simon.

Simon (*coming down to* **Sorel**)   And I wish you'd confine your girlish infatuations to London, and not force them on your defenceless family.

Sorel   I shall keep him out of your way as much as possible.

Simon   Do, darling. (*Goes to piano and lights cigarette.*)

Enter **Clara** *from door below stairs. She is a hot, round, untidy little woman. She stands L. by door.*

Simon (*sits on form by piano*)   Clara, has Mother asked anyone down this week-end?

Clara   I don't know, dear. There isn't much food in the house, and Amy's got toothache.

Sorel   I've got some oil of cloves somewhere.

Clara   She tried that, but it only burnt her tongue. The poor girl's been writhing about in the scullery like one o'clock.

Sorel   You haven't forgotten to put those flowers in the

Japanese room?

Simon   The Japanese room is essentially feminine, and entirely unsuited to the Pet of the Foreign Office.

Sorel   Shut up, Simon!

Clara   The room looks lovely, dear – you needn't worry. Just like your mother's dressing-room on a first night.

Simon   How restful!

Clara (*moves to* **Sorel**)   Have you told her about your boy friend?

Sorel (*pained*)   Not boy friend, Clara.

Clara (*picks up drawing that* **Simon** *has left on floor C.*)   Oh, well, whatever he is. (*Puts drawing on chair up C.*)

Simon   I think Sorel's beginning to be ashamed of us all, Clara – I don't altogether blame her; we are very slap-dash.

Clara (*coming down C. – speaking to* **Simon**)   Are you going to leave that picture in the guests' bathroom, dear? I don't know if it's quite the thing – lots of pink, naked women rolling about in a field.

Simon (*severely*)   Nudity can be very beautiful, Clara.

Clara   Oh, can it! Perhaps being a dresser for so long 'as spoilt me eye for it.

Clara *goes out door below stairs.*

Simon   Clara's looking tired. We ought to have more servants and not depend on her so much.

Sorel   You know we can never keep them. You're right about us being slap-dash, Simon. I wish we weren't.

Simon   Does it matter?

Sorel   It must, I think – to other people.

Simon   It's not our fault – it's the way we've been brought up.

Sorel Well, if we're clever enough to realise that, we ought to be clever enough to change ourselves.

Simon I'm not sure that I want to.

Sorel We're so awfully bad-mannered.

Simon Not to people we like.

Sorel The people we like put up with it because they like *us*.

Simon What do you mean, exactly, by bad manners? Lack of social tricks and small-talk?

Sorel We never attempt to look after people when they come here.

Simon Why should we? It's loathsome being looked after.

Sorel Yes, but people like little attentions. We've never once asked anyone if they've slept well.

Simon I consider *that* an impertinence, anyhow.

Sorel I'm going to try to improve.

Simon (*puts feet upon form*) You're only going on like this because you've got a mania for a diplomatist. You'll soon return to normal.

Sorel (*earnestly*) Abnormal, Simon – that's what we are. Abnormal. People stare in astonishment when we say what we consider perfectly ordinary things. I just remarked at Freda's lunch the other day how nice it would be if someone invented something to make all our faces go up like the Chinese, because I was so bored with them going down. And they all thought I was mad!

Simon It's no use worrying, darling; we see things differently, I suppose, and if people don't like it they must lump it.

Enter **Judith** *from the garden. She is carrying an armful of flowers and wearing a tea-gown, a large garden hat, gauntlet gloves and galoshes.*

Judith (*coming down to behind sofa table*)   You look awfully dirty, Simon. What have you been doing?

Simon (*nonchalantly*)   Not washing very much.

Judith (*puts basket on table, and starts to take off gloves*)   You should, darling, really. It's so bad for your skin to leave things about on it.

Sorel   Clara says Amy's got toothache.

Judith   Poor dear! There's some oil of cloves in my medicine cupboard. Who is Amy?

Sorel   The scullery-maid, I think.

Judith (*puts gloves on table and comes C.*)   How extraordinary! She doesn't look Amy a bit, does she? Much more Flossie. Give me a cigarette.

Simon *gives her a cigarette from box on piano.*

Judith   Delphiniums are those stubby red flowers, aren't they?

Simon (*lights cigarette for* **Judith**)   No, darling; they're tall and blue.

Judith   Yes, of course. The red ones are somebody's name – Asters, that's it. I knew it was something opulent. (*Sits on stool below piano.* **Simon** *takes off her galoshes and puts them by the side of the stool.*) I do hope Clara has remembered about the Japanese room.

Sorel   Japanese room!

Judith   Yes; I told her to put some flowers in it and take Simon's flannels out of the wardrobe drawer.

Sorel   So did I.

Judith (*ominously*)   Why?

Sorel (*airily*)   I've asked Richard Greatham down for the week-end – I didn't think you'd mind.

Judith (*rises and crosses to* **Sorel**)   Mind! How dared you do such a thing?

Sorel   He's a diplomatist.

Judith (*goes behind table and starts to sort out flowers*)   That makes it much worse. We must wire and put him off at once.

Sorel   It's too late.

Judith   Well, we'll tell Clara to say we've been called away.

Sorel   That would be extremely rude, and, anyhow, I *want* to see him.

Judith   You mean to sit there in cold blood and tell me you've asked a complete stranger down for the week-end, and that you *want* to see him!

Sorel   I've often done it before.

Judith   I fail to see how that helps matters. Where's he going to sleep?

Sorel   The Japanese room.

Judith (*crosses with bunch of flowers to table below door R.*)   Oh, no, he isn't – Sandy Tyrell is sleeping there.

Simon (*coming C.*)   There now! What did I tell you?

Sorel   Sandy – what?

Judith   Tyrell, dear.

Simon   Why didn't you tell us, Mother?

Judith (*starting to arrange flowers in vase*)   I did. I've talked of nothing but Sandy Tyrell for days – I adore Sandy Tyrell.

Simon (*goes back to form and sits*)   You've never mentioned him.

Sorel   Who is he, Mother?

Judith   He's a perfect darling, and madly in love with me – at least, it isn't me really, it's my Celebrated Actress glamour – but it gives me a divinely cosy feeling. I met him at Nora Trent's. (*Crosses to behind sofa table.*)

Sorel   Mother, I wish you'd give up this sort of thing.

Judith (*taking more flowers from basket*)   What exactly do you mean by 'this sort of thing', Sorel?

Sorel   You know perfectly well what I mean.

Judith (*puts down flowers and goes to R. corner of sofa*)   Are you attempting to criticize me?

Sorel   I should have thought you'd be above encouraging silly, callow young men who are infatuated by your name.

Judith (*goes back to table and picks up flowers*)   That may be true, but I shall allow nobody but myself to say it. I hoped you'd grow up a good *daughter* to me, not a critical *aunt*.

Sorel (*moves to L. end of sofa*)   It's so terribly cheap.

Judith   Cheap! Nonsense! How about your diplomatist?

Sorel   Surely that's a little different, dear?

Judith   If you mean that because you happen to be a vigorous *ingénue* of nineteen you have the complete monopoly of any amorous adventure there may be about, I feel it my firm duty to disillusion you.

Sorel   But, Mother—

Judith (*crosses to top end of piano and picks up empty vase, which she gives* **Simon** *to hold while she fills it with flowers*)   Anyone would think I was eighty, the way you go on. It was a great mistake not sending you to boarding schools, and you coming back and me being your elder sister.

Simon   It wouldn't have been any use, darling. Everyone knows we're your son and daughter.

Judith   Only because I was stupid enough to dandle you about in front of cameras when you were little. I knew I should regret it.

Simon   I don't see any point in trying to be younger than you are.

Judith   At your age, dear, it would be indecent if you did.

Having finished arranging flowers, she puts vase back on piano, and crosses to R. corner of sofa.

Sorel   But, Mother darling, don't you see it's awfully undignified for you to go flaunting about with young men?

Judith   I don't flaunt about – I never have. I've been morally an extremely nice woman all my life – more or less – and if dabbling gives me pleasure, I don't see why I *shouldn't* dabble.

Sorel   But it *oughtn't* to give you pleasure any *more*.

Judith   You know, Sorel, you grow more damnably feminine every day. I wish I'd brought you up differently.

Sorel   I'm proud of being feminine.

Judith (*sits on sofa beside* **Sorel** *– kissing her*)   You're a darling, and I adore you; and you're very pretty, and I'm madly jealous of you.

Sorel (*with her arms round her*)   Are you really? How lovely!

Judith   You will be nice to Sandy, won't you?

Sorel (*sits up*)   Can't he sleep in 'Little Hell'?

Judith   My dear, he's frightfully athletic and all those hot-water pipes will sap his vitality.

Sorel   They'll sap Richard's vitality too.

Judith   He won't notice them; he's probably used to scorching tropical Embassies with punkahs waving and everything.

Simon   He's sure to be deadly, anyhow.

Sorel   You're getting far too blasé and exclusive, Simon.

Simon   Nothing of the sort. Only I loathe being hearty with your men friends.

Sorel You've never been even civil to any of my friends, men or women.

Judith Don't bicker.

Simon (*rises and crosses to C.*) Anyhow, the Japanese room's a woman's room, and a woman ought to have it.

Judith I promised it to Sandy – he loves anything Japanese.

Simon So does Myra!

Judith Myra!

Simon Myra Arundel. I've asked her down.

Judith You've – what!

Simon I've asked Myra down for the week-end – she's awfully amusing.

Sorel Well, all I can say is, it's beastly of you. You might have warned me. What on earth will Richard say?

Simon Something exquisitely non-committal, I expect.

Judith This is too much! Do you mean to tell me, Simon—

Simon (*goes to* **Judith** *– firmly*) Yes, Mother, I do. I've asked Myra down and I have a perfect right to. You've always brought us up to be free about things.

Judith Myra Arundel is straining freedom to its *utmost* limits.

Simon Don't you like her?

Judith No, dear, I detest her. She's far too old for you, and she goes about using sex as a sort of shrimping-net.

Simon Really, Mother—!

Judith It's no use being cross. You know perfectly well I dislike her, and that's why you never told me she was coming until too late to stop her. It's intolerable of you.

Sorel (*grandly*) Whether she's here or not is a matter of extreme indifference to *me*, but I'm afraid Richard won't like her very much.

Simon You're afraid he'll like her *too* much!

Sorel That was an offensive remark, Simon, and rather silly.

Judith (*plaintively*) Why on earth don't you fall in love with nice young girls, instead of self-conscious vampires?

Simon She's not a vampire, and I never said I was in love with her.

Sorel He's crazy about her. She butters him up and admires his sketches.

Simon (*leaning across* **Judith** *and shouting at* **Sorel**) What about you picking up old gentlemen at dances?

Sorel (*furiously – shouting back at him*) He's *not* old!

Judith (*stretches her arms up and parts them;* **Simon** *goes C.*) You've both upset me thoroughly. I wanted a nice restful week-end, with moments of Sandy's ingenuous affection to warm the cockles of my heart when I felt in the mood, and now the house is going to be full of discord – not enough food, everyone fighting for the bath – perfect agony! I wish I were dead!

Simon You needn't worry about Myra and me. We shall keep out of everyone's way.

Sorel I shall take Richard on the river all day to-morrow.

Judith In what?

Sorel The punt.

Judith I absolutely forbid you to go near the punt.

Simon It's sure to rain, anyhow.

Judith What your father will say I tremble to think. He needs complete quiet to finish off *The Sinful Woman*.

Sorel I see no reason for there to be any noise, unless Sandy What's-his-name is given to shouting.

Judith If you're rude to Sandy I shall be extremely angry.

Simon *and* **Sorel** *bend over* **Judith** *and all talk loudly at once.*

Sorel		Now, look here, Mother—
Simon	*(together)*	Why you should expect—
Judith		He's coming all the way down specially to be nice to me—

Enter **David** *down stairs. He looks slightly irritable.*

David *(coming down to C.)* Why are you all making such a noise?

Simon *crosses to piano and picks up book.*

Judith I think I'm going mad!

David Why hasn't Clara brought me my tea?

Judith I don't know.

David Where is Clara?

Judith Do stop firing questions at me, David.

David Why are you all so irritable? What's happened?

Enter **Clara** *from below stairs, with a tray of tea for one, and thrusts it into* **David**'s *hands.*

Clara Here's your tea. I'm sorry I'm late with it. Amy forgot to put the kettle on – she's got terrible toothache.

David Poor girl! Give her some oil of cloves.

Sorel If anyone else mentions oil of cloves, I shall do something desperate! *(Rises and moves a step L.)*

David It's wonderful stuff. Where's Zoe?

Simon She was in the garden this morning.

David   I suppose no one thought of giving her any lunch?

Clara   I put it down by the kitchen table as usual, but she never came in for it.

Sorel   She's probably mousing.

David   She isn't old enough yet. She might have fallen into the river, for all you care. I think it's a shame!

Clara   Don't you worry your head – Zoe won't come to any harm; she's too wily.

Exit door below stairs.

David   I don't want to be disturbed. (*He takes his tray and goes upstairs; then he turns.*) Listen, Simon. There's a perfectly sweet flapper coming down by the four-thirty. Will you go and meet her and be nice to her? She's an abject fool, but a useful type, and I want to study her a little in domestic surroundings. She can sleep in the Japanese room.

He goes off, leaving behind him a deathly silence. **Sorel** *drops into chair down L.*

Judith (*pause*)   I should like someone to play something very beautiful to me on the piano.

Simon (*stamps up to french window C.*)   Damn everything! Damn! Damn! Damn!

Sorel   Swearing doesn't help.

Simon   It helps me a lot.

Sorel   What does Father mean by going on like that?

Judith   In view of the imminent reception, you'd better go and shave, Simon.

Simon *comes down and leans on piano.*

Sorel (*rising and bursting into tears of rage*)   It's perfectly beastly! Whenever I make any sort of plan about anything, it's always done in by someone. I wish I were earning my own living somewhere – a free agent – able to do whatever I liked without being cluttered up and frustrated by the family—

Judith (*picturesquely*) It grieves me to hear you say that, Sorel.

Sorel Don't be infuriating, Mother!

Judith (*sadly*) A change has come over my children of late. I have tried to shut my eyes to it, but in vain. At my time of life one must face bitter facts!

Simon This is going to be the blackest Saturday-till-Monday we've ever spent!

Judith (*tenderly*) Sorel, you mustn't cry.

Sorel Don't sympathise with me; it's only temper.

Judith (*pulling her down on to sofa beside her*) Put your head on my shoulder, dear.

Simon (*bitterly*) Your head, like the golden fleece . . .

Sorel (*tearfully*) Richard'll have to have 'Little Hell' and that horrible flapper the Japanese room.

Judith Over my dead body!

Simon (*comes over to his mother*) Mother, what *are* we to do?

Judith (*pulls him down on his knees and places his head on her right shoulder.* **Sorel**'s *head on her left. Makes a charming little motherly picture*) We must all be very, very kind to everyone!

Simon Now then, Mother, none of that!

Judith (*aggrieved*) I don't know what you mean, Simon.

Simon You were being beautiful and sad.

Judith But I am beautiful and sad.

Simon You're not particularly beautiful, darling, and you never were.

Judith Never mind; I made thousands think I was.

Simon And as for being sad—

Judith (*pushes* **Simon** *on the floor*)   Now, Simon, I will not be dictated to like this! If I say I'm sad, I *am* sad. You don't understand, because you're precocious and tiresome. . . . There comes a time in all women's lives—

Sorel (*rises and stands at L. corner of sofa*)   Oh dear! (*With pained expression.*)

Judith   What did you say, Sorel?

Sorel   I said, 'Oh dear!'

Judith   Well, please don't say it again, because it annoys me.

Sorel (*smiling*)   You're such a lovely hypocrite!

Judith (*casting up her eyes*)   I don't know what I've done to be cursed with such ungrateful children! It's very cruel at my time of life—

Simon   There you go again!

Judith (*pause – inconsequently*)   You're getting far too tall, Sorel.

Sorel   Sorry, Mother!

Judith   Give me another of those disgusting cigarettes—

Simon *rises and goes to piano – quickly takes cigarette.*

Judith   I don't know where they came from. (*Rises and goes C.*)

Simon (*moves C. and gives* **Judith** *cigarette*)   Here! (*He lights it for her.*)

Judith   I'm going to forget entirely about all these dreadful people arriving. My mind henceforward shall be a blank on the subject.

Sorel   It's all very fine, Mother, but—

Judith   I made a great decision this morning.

Simon   What kind of decision?

Judith It's a secret.

Sorel Aren't you going to tell us?

Judith Of course. I meant it was a secret from your father.

Simon What is it?

Judith *goes up C. and looks off L. to make sure no one is listening, then returns to C.*

Judith I'm going back to the stage.

Simon I knew it! (*Drops on to form below piano.*)

Judith I'm stagnating here. I won't stagnate as long as there's breath left in my body.

Sorel Do you think it's wise? You retired so very finally last year. What excuse will you give for returning so soon?

Judith My public, dear – letters from my public!

Simon Have you had any?

Judith One or two. That's what decided me, really – I ought to have had hundreds.

Sorel (*kneels on R. corner of sofa*) We'll write some lovely ones, and you can publish them in the papers.

Judith Of course.

Sorel You will be dignified about it all, won't you, darling?

Judith I'm much more dignified on the stage than in the country – it's my *milieu*. I've tried terribly hard to be 'landed gentry', but without any real success. (*Moves up C. with outstretched arms.*) I long for excitement and glamour. (*Comes down to R. corner of sofa.*) Think of the thrill of a first night; all those ardent playgoers willing one to succeed; the critics all leaning forward with glowing faces, receptive and exultant – emitting queer little inarticulate noises as some witty line tickles their fancy. The satisfied grunt of the *Daily Mail*, the abandoned gurgle of the *Sunday Times*, and the shrill, enthusiastic scream of the *Daily Express!* I can distinguish them all—

Simon Have you got a play?

Judith I think I shall revive *Love's Whirlwind.*

Sorel (*collapsing on to sofa*) Oh, Mother! (*She gurgles with laughter.*)

Simon (*weakly*) Father will be furious.

Judith I can't help that.

Sorel It's such a fearful play.

Judith It's a marvellous part.

Sorel *opens her mouth to speak.*

Judith You mustn't say too much against it, Sorel. I'm willing to laugh at it a little myself, but, after all, it *was* one of my greatest successes.

Simon Oh, it's appalling – but I love it. It makes me laugh.

Judith The public love it too, and it doesn't make them laugh – much. (*Moves to C. and very dramatically she recites.*) 'You are a fool, a blind pitiable fool. You think because you have bought my body that you have bought my soul!' (*Turning to* **Sorel**.) You must say that's dramatic – 'I've dreamed of love like this, but I never realized, I never knew how beautiful it could be in reality!' (*Wipes away imaginary tears.*) That line always brought a tear to my eye.

Simon The second act *is* the best, there's no doubt about that.

Judith (*turning to* **Sorel**) From the moment Victor comes in it's strong – tremendously strong. . . . Be Victor a minute, Sorel—

Sorel (*rising*) Do you mean when he comes in at the end of the act?

Judith Yes. You know – 'Is this a game?'

Sorel (*going to* **Judith** *and speaking in a very dramatic voice*) 'Is this a game?'

Judith (*with spirit*)   'Yes – and a game that must be played to the finish.'

Simon (*rising and moving to* **Judith**, *and speaking in deep dramatic voice*)   'Zara, what does this mean?'

Judith   'So many illusions shattered – so many dreams trodden in the dust!'

Sorel (*runs behind* **Judith** *and in front of* **Simon** *to down R.*)   I'm George now – 'I don't understand! You and Victor – My God!' (*Strikes dramatic pose.*)

Judith (*moving a little to L. – listening*)   'Sssh! Isn't that little Pam crying?'

Simon (*savagely*)   'She'll cry more, poor mite, when she realizes her mother is a—'

The front-door bell rings.

Judith   Damn! There's the bell!

Sorel (*rushing to the glass – on piano*)   I look hideous.

Simon (*moves to R. side of piano*)   Yes, dear!

Clara *enters from door below stairs and crosses to door R.*

Judith   Clara – before you open the door – we shall be eight for dinner.

Clara (*comes to R.C.*)   My God!

Simon   And for breakfast, lunch tea, and dinner to-morrow.

Judith (*vaguely*)   Will you get various rooms ready?

Clara   I shall have to – they can't sleep in the passage!

Sorel   Now we've upset Clara!

Judith   It can't be helped – nothing can be helped. It's Fate – everything that happens is Fate. That's always a great comfort to me.

Clara More like arrant selfishness!

Judith You mustn't be pert, Clara.

Clara Pert I may be, but I 'ave got some thought for others. Eight for dinner – Amy going home early! It's nothing more nor less than an imposition!

The bell rings again.

Simon Hadn't you better let them all in?

Clara *goes to the front door and admits* **Sandy Tyrell**, *who is a fresh-looking young man; he has an unspoilt, youthful sense of honour and rather big hands, owing to a misplaced enthusiasm for amateur boxing.*

Clara *goes out, door below stairs.*

Sandy (*crossing to* **Judith** *and shaking hands*) I say, it's perfectly ripping of you to let me come down.

Judith Are you alone?

Sandy (*surprised*) Yes.

Judith I mean, didn't you meet anyone at the station?

Sandy I motored down; my car's outside. Would you like me to meet anybody?

Judith Oh, no, I must introduce you. This is my daughter Sorel, and my son Simon.

Sandy (*moves to* **Sorel** *and offers his hand, which she ignores*) How do you do?

Sorel (*coldly*) I'm extremely well, thank you, and I hope you are.

Brushes past him and exits upstairs.

Simon So do I. (*Does the same.*)

Sandy *looks shattered.*

Judith (*crosses in front of* **Sandy** *and glares after* **Simon** *and*

Sorel.) You must forgive me for having rather peculiar children. Have you got a bag or anything?

Sandy Yes; it's in the car.

Judith We'd better leave it there for the moment, as Clara has to get the tea. We'll find you a room afterwards.

Sandy I've been looking forward to this most awfully.

Judith It is nice, isn't it? (*Moves to window.*) You can see as far as Marlow on a clear day, so they tell me.

Sandy (*goes up to her*) I meant I've been looking forward to seeing you.

Judith How perfectly sweet of you! (*Crosses to sofa and sits L. corner.*) Would you like a drink?

Sandy No, thanks. I'm in training.

Judith (*motioning him to sit beside her*) How lovely! What for?

Sandy I'm boxing again in a couple of weeks.

Judith I must come to your first night.

Sandy (*sits on sofa*) You look simply splendid.

Judith I'm so glad. You know, you mustn't mind if Simon and Sorel insult you a little – they've been very bad-tempered lately.

Sandy It's awfully funny you having a grown-up son and daughter at all. I can hardly believe it.

Judith (*quickly*) I was married very young.

Sandy I don't wonder. You know, it's frightfully queer the way I've been planning to know you for ages, and I never did until last week.

Judith I liked you from the first, really, because you're such a nice shape.

Sandy (*slightly embarrassed*) Oh, I see. . . .

Judith Small hips and lovely broad shoulders – I wish

Simon had smaller hips. (*Slight pause.*) Do you think you could teach him to box?

Sandy   Rather – if he likes!

Judith   That's just the trouble – I'm afraid he won't like. He's so dreadfully un – that sort of thing. You must use your influence subtly. I'm sure David would be pleased.

Sandy   Who's David?

Judith   My husband.

Sandy (*surprised*)   Oh!

Judith   Why do you say 'Oh' like that? Didn't you know I had a husband?

Sandy   I thought he was dead.

Judith   No, he's not dead; he's upstairs. (*Pointing to stairs.*)

Sandy   You're quite different from what you were the other day.

Judith   It's this garden hat. I'll take it off. (*She does so and puts it on table behind sofa.*) There! I've been pruning the calceolarias.

Sandy (*puzzled*)   Oh?—

Judith   I love my garden, you know – it's so peaceful and quaint. I spend long days dreaming away in it – you know how one dreams.

Sandy   Oh, yes.

Judith (*warming up*)   I always longed to leave the brittle glamour of cities and theatres and find rest in some old-world nook. That's why we came to Cookham.

Sandy   Awfully nice place, Cookham.

Judith (*slight pause*)   Have you ever seen me on the stage?

Sandy   Rather!

Judith   Oh, what in?

Sandy   That thing when you pretended to cheat at cards to save your husband's good name.

Judith   Oh, *The Bold Deceiver*. That play was never quite right.

Sandy   You were absolutely wonderful. That was when I first fell in love with you.

Judith (*delighted*)   Was it, really?

Sandy   Yes; you were so frightfully pathetic and brave.

Judith (*basking*)   Was I?

Sandy   Rather!

There is a pause.

Judith   Well, go on. . . .

Sandy (*flustered*)   I feel such a fool, telling you what I think, as though it mattered.

Judith   Of course it matters – to me, anyhow.

Sandy   Does it – honestly?

Judith   Certainly.

Sandy   It seems too good to be true – sitting here and talking as though we were old friends.

Judith   We *are* old friends – we probably met in another life. Reincarnation, you know – fascinating!

Sandy   You do say ripping things.

Judith   Do I? Give me a cigarette.

He takes cigarette from box on table and gives it to her.

And let's put our feet up. (*She puts her feet up behind **Sandy**, and he lights her cigarette.*)

Sandy   All right.

They settle themselves comfortably at opposite ends of the sofa, smoking.

Judith Can you punt?

Sandy Yes – a bit.

Judith You must teach Simon – he always gets the pole stuck.

Sandy I'd rather teach you.

Judith You're so gallant and chivalrous – much more like an American than an Englishman.

Sandy I should like to go on saying nice things to you for ever.

Judith (*giving him her hand*) Sandy!

There comes a loud ring at the bell.

There now! (*Takes her feet off sofa.*)

Sandy Is anyone else coming to stay?

Judith Anyone else! You don't know – you just don't know.

Clara *enters and crosses over to door R., opens it and lets it fall back in* **Myra***'s face, then exits, L.*

Sandy You said it would be quite quiet, with nobody at all.

Judith I was wrong. It's going to be very noisy, with herds of angry people stamping about. Give me my hat.

He gives her her hat, which she puts on.

Myra *pushes open door, and puts her suitcase and tennis racket just outside door, and enters, coming to C. and holding out her hand to* **Judith***.*

Sandy *rises.*

Myra (*advancing*) Judith – my dear – this is divine!

Judith (*rises and meets* **Myra***, C. – emptily*) Too, too lovely! Where are the others?

Myra What others?

Judith Did you come by the four-thirty?

Myra Yes.

Judith Didn't you see anyone at the station?

Myra Yes, several people, but I didn't know they were coming here.

Judith Well, they are.

Myra Sorel said it was going to be just ourselves this week-end.

Judith (*sharply*) Sorel?

Myra Yes – didn't she tell you she'd asked me? Weren't you expecting me?

Judith Simon muttered something about your coming, but Sorel didn't mention it. (*Looks at* **Myra** *and gives a chuckle.*) Wasn't that odd of her? (*Crosses to piano.*)

Myra You're a divinely mad family! (*To* **Sandy**.) How do you do? It's useless to wait for introductions, with the Blisses. My name's Myra Arundel.

Judith (*airily*) Sandy Tyrell, Myra Arundel; Myra Arundel, Sandy Tyrell. There!

Myra Is that your car outside?

Sandy Yes.

Myra (*moving to* **Judith** *again*) Well, Judith, I *do* think you might have told me someone was motoring down. A nice car would have been so much more comfortable than that beastly train.

Judith I never knew you were coming until a little while ago.

Myra It's heavenly here – after London! The heat was terrible when I left. You look awfully well, Judith. Rusticating obviously agrees with you.

Judith I'm glad you think so. Personally, I feel that a nervous breakdown is imminent.

Myra My dear, how ghastly! What's the matter?

Judith Nothing's the matter yet, Myra, but I have presentiments. (*Crosses in front of* **Myra** *and takes* **Sandy**'s *hand. She begins to go upstairs, followed by* **Sandy**. *Then she turns.*) Come upstairs, Sandy, and I'll show you your room. I'll send Simon down to you. He's shaving, I think, but you won't mind that, will you?

She goes off. **Myra** *makes a slight grimace after her, then she helps herself to a cigarette and wanders to piano.*

Simon *comes downstairs very fast, putting on his coat. He has apparently finished his toilet.*

Simon (*runs over to* **Myra**) Myra, this is marvellous! (*He tries to kiss her.*)

Myra (*pushing him away*) No, Simon, dear; it's too hot.

Simon You look beautifully cool.

Myra I'm more than cool, really, but it's not climatic coolness. I've been mentally chilled to the marrow by Judith's attitude.

Simon Why, what did she say?

Myra Nothing very much. She was bouncing about on the sofa with a hearty young thing in flannels, and seemed to resent my appearance rather.

Simon You mustn't take any notice of Mother.

Myra I'll try not to, but it's difficult.

Simon She adores you, really.

Myra I'm sure she does.

Simon She's annoyed to-day because Father and Sorel have been asking people down without telling her.

Myra Poor dear! I quite see why.

Simon You look enchanting!

Myra   Thank you, Simon.

Simon   Are you pleased to see me?

Myra   Of course. That's why I came.

Simon (*shouts*)   Darling!

Myra   Sssh! Don't shout.

Simon (*moving away to C.*)   I feel most colossally temperamental – I should like to kiss you and kiss you and break everything in the house and then jump into the river.

Myra   Dear Simon!

Simon (*he takes her hand and studies her*)   You're everything I want you to be – absolutely everything! Marvellous clothes, marvellous looks, marvellous brain – oh, God, it's terrible! (*Drops her hand and moves L.*)

Myra   I dined with Charlie Templeton last night.

Simon   Well, you're a devil! You only did it to annoy me. He's far too plump, and he can't do anything but dither about the Embassy in badly-cut trousers. You loathe him really; you know you do – you're too intelligent not to. You couldn't like him and me at the same time – it's impossible!

Myra   Don't be so conceited.

Simon (*running to her and clasping her in his arms*)   Darling – I adore you!

Myra   That's right.

Simon (*releasing her*)   But you're callous – that's what it is, callous! You don't care a damn. You don't love me a bit, do you?

Myra   Love's a very big word, Simon.

Simon   It isn't – it's tiny. What are we to do?

Myra   What do you mean?

Simon   We can't go on like this.

Myra   I'm not going on like anything. (*Crosses over and sits in chair down L.*)

Simon   Yes, you are; you're going on like Medusa, and there are awful snakes popping their heads out at me from under your hat – I shall be turned to stone in a minute, and then you'll be sorry.

Myra (*laughing*)   You're very sweet, and I'm *very* fond of you.

Simon (*crosses over to her and takes her hand*)   Tell me what you've been doing – everything.

Myra   Nothing.

Simon   What did you do after you'd dined with Charlie Templeton?

Myra   Supped with Charlie Templeton.

Simon   Well! (*Throws her hand down and goes to R. corner of sofa and sits on arm.*) I don't mind a bit. I hope you ate a lot and enjoyed yourself – there!

Myra   Generous boy! Come and kiss me.

Simon   You're only playing up to me now; you don't really want to a bit.

Myra   I'm aching for it.

Simon (*runs to her and kisses her violently*)   I love you!

Myra   This week-end's going to be strenuous.

Simon (*moves away to C.*)   Hell upon earth – fifteen million people in the house. We'll get up at seven and rush away down the river.

Myra   No, we won't.

Simon   Well, don't let either of us agree to anything we say – we'll both be difficult. (*Flings himself on sofa with his feet up on L. end.*) I love being difficult.

Myra   You certainly do.

Simon   But I'm in the most lovely mood now. Just seeing you makes me feel grand—

Myra   Is your father here?

Simon   Yes; he's working on a new novel.

Myra   He writes brilliantly.

Simon   Doesn't he? He drinks too much tea, though.

Myra   It can't do him much harm, surely?

Simon   It tans the stomach.

Myra   Who is Sandy Tyrell?

Simon   Never heard of him.

Myra   He's here, with Judith.

Simon   Oh, *that* poor thing with hot hands! We'll ignore him.

Myra   I thought he looked rather nice.

Simon   You must be mad! He looked disgusting.

Myra (*laughing*)   Idiot!

Simon   Smooth my hair with your soft white hands.

Myra (*rises and goes to R. end of sofa – ruffling it*)   It's got glue on it.

Simon (*catching her hand and kissing it*)   You smell heavenly! What is it?

Myra   Borgia of Rosine.

Simon   How appropriate! (*He tries to pull her down and kiss her.*)

Myra (*breaking away*)   You're too demonstrative to-day, Simon.

The front-door bell rings.

Simon   Damn, damn! It's those drearies. (*Takes his feet off sofa.*)

Clara *enters, crosses to door R., opens it and lets it fall back in* **Richard**'s *face, and starts to return to door L., but stops as he speaks.* **Richard Greatham** *and* **Jackie Coryton** *come in. There is, by this time, a good deal of luggage on the step.* **Richard** *is iron-grey and tall;* **Jackie** *is small and shingled, with an ingenuous manner which will lose its charm as she grows older.*

Richard   Is this Mrs Bliss's house?

Clara *(off-hand)*   Oh, yes, this is it.

Richard   Is Miss Sorel Bliss in?

Clara   I expect so. I'll see if I can find her.

She goes upstairs.

Richard *closes door.* **Jackie** *goes down R.*

Simon *(rises and crosses to* **Richard***, carelessly shakes hands, then turns back to* **Myra***, ignoring* **Richard***)*   Hallo! Did you have a nice journey?

Richard   Yes thank you, very nice. I met Miss Coryton at the station. We introduced ourselves while we were waiting for the only taxi to come back.

Myra *(taking a step down L.C.)*   Oh, *I* took the only taxi. How maddening of me!

Richard *(crosses to her and shakes hands)*   Mrs Arundel! How do you do? I never recognised you.

Simon *goes behind* **Richard** *to R.C. and stares at* **Jackie** *rudely.*

Jackie   I did.

Myra   Why? Have we met anywhere?

Jackie   No; I mean I recognised you as the one who took the taxi.

Richard *(to* **Simon***)*   You are Sorel's brother?

Simon   Yes; she'll be down in a minute. Come out into the garden, Myra—

Myra But, Simon, we can't. . . .

Simon (*reaching across* **Richard**, *grabbing her hand and dragging her off through window*) Yes, we can. I shall go mad if I stay in the house a moment longer. (*Over his shoulder to* **Richard** *and* **Jackie**.) Tea will be here soon.

He and **Myra** *go off into garden R.*

There's a slight pause.

Jackie Well!

Richard A strange young man! (*Moving up to window, looking after them.*)

Jackie Very rude, *I* think.

Richard (*turning back into the room*) Have you ever met him before?

Jackie No; I don't know any of them except Mr Bliss – *he's* a wonderful person.

Richard (*puts his coat and hat on chair up L.C.*) I wonder if he knows you're here.

Jackie Perhaps that funny woman who opened the door will tell him.

Richard Yes, allow me. (*Takes her coat and puts it on chair with his.*) It was fortunate that we met at the station.

Jackie I'm frightfully glad. I should have been terrified arriving all by myself.

Richard (*looks out of window again. Slight pause*) I do hope the weather will keep good over Sunday – the country round here is delightful.

Jackie Yes.

Another pause.

Richard There's nowhere like England in the spring and summer.

Jackie No, there isn't, is there?

Another pause.

Richard   There's a sort of *quality* you find in no other countries.

Another pause, in which **Jackie** *moves over to sofa and sits.*

Jackie   Have you travelled a lot?

Richard (*modestly*)   A good deal.

Jackie   How lovely!

Richard *comes down and sits on form below piano.*

There is a pause.

Richard   Spain is very beautiful.

Jackie   Yes, I've always heard Spain was awfully nice.

Pause.

Richard   Except for the bull-fights. No one who ever really loved horses could enjoy a bull-fight.

Jackie   Nor anyone who loved bulls either.

Richard   Exactly.

Pause.

Jackie   Italy's awfully nice, isn't it?

Richard   Oh, yes, charming.

Jackie   I've always wanted to go to Italy.

Pause.

Richard   Rome is a beautiful city.

Jackie   Yes, I've always heard Rome was lovely.

Richard   And Naples and Capri – Capri's enchanting.

Jackie   It must be.

Pause.

Richard   Have you ever been abroad at all?

Jackie   Oh, yes: I went to Dieppe once – we had a house there for the summer.

Richard (*kindly*)   Dear little place, Dieppe.

Jackie   Yes, it was lovely.

Judith *comes downstairs, followed by* **Sandy**, *with his arms full of cushions. Sits down on form and puts on her galoshes beside* **Richard**, *who rises. Then exits into garden without looking at* **Richard** *or* **Jackie**. **Sandy** *picks up cushions and her gloves from table and goes out after her.*

Jackie   Well!

Pause, and sitting again.

Richard   *Russia* used to be a wonderful country before the war.

Jackie   It must have been. . . . Was that her?

Richard   Who?

Jackie   Judith Bliss.

Richard   Yes, I expect it was.

Jackie (*nearly crying*)   I wish I'd never come.

Richard   You mustn't worry. They're a very Bohemian family, I believe.

Jackie   I wonder if Mr Bliss knows I'm here.

Richard   I wonder.

Jackie   Couldn't we ring a bell, or anything?

Richard   Yes, perhaps we'd better. (*Rises and crosses to door down L. He finds bell and presses it.*)

Jackie   I don't suppose it rings.

Richard (*comes to L. corner of sofa*)   You mustn't be depressed.

Jackie   I feel horrid.

Richard   It's always a little embarrassing coming to a strange house for the first time. You'll like Sorel – she's charming.

Jackie (*desperately*)   I wonder where she is.

Richard (*consolingly*)   I expect tea will be here soon.

Jackie   Do you think they *have* tea?

Richard (*alarmed*)   Oh, yes – they must.

Jackie   Oh, well, we'd better go on waiting, then.

Richard (*takes cigarette-case out of his pocket*)   Do you mind if I smoke?

Jackie   Not a bit.

Richard   Will you?

Jackie   No, thank you.

Richard (*sitting down on L. end of sofa*)   I got this case in Japan. It's pretty isn't it?

Jackie (*takes case, turns it over and hands it back*)   Awfully pretty.

They lapse into hopeless silence.

Enter **Sorel** *downstairs – comes to L.C.*

Sorel   Oh, Richard, I'm dreadfully sorry! I didn't know you were here. (*They shake hands.*)

Richard   We've been here a good while.

Sorel   How awful! Please forgive me. I was upstairs.

Jackie *bobs up under their hands and stands in front of* **Richard**.

Richard   This is Miss Coryton.

Sorel   Oh!

Jackie   How do you do?

Sorel   Have you come to see Father?

Richard *lights his cigarette.*

Jackie Yes.

Sorel He's in his study. (*Moves away to C.*) You'd better go up.

Jackie (*looks hopelessly at* **Richard**, *then goes to* **Sorel** *and clutches her arm*) I don't know the way.

Sorel (*irritably*) Oh, well – I'll take you. Come on! Wait a minute, Richard. (*She takes her to the bottom of the stairs.*) It's along that passage and the third door on the right.

Jackie Oh, thank you. (*She goes upstairs despondently.*)

Sorel (*coming down again – to* **Richard**) The poor girl looks half-witted.

Richard She's shy, I think.

Sorel I hope Father will find her a comfort. (*Sits on R. end of sofa.*)

Richard Tell me one thing, Sorel, did your father and mother know I was coming? (*Sits beside her.*)

Sorel Oh, yes; they were awfully pleased.

Richard A rather nice-looking woman came down, in a big hat, and went into the garden with a young man, without saying a word.

Sorel That was Mother, I expect. We're an independent family – we entertain our friends sort of separately.

Richard Oh, I see.

Slight pause.

Sorel It was sweet of you to come.

Richard I wanted to come – I've thought about you a lot.

Sorel Have you really? That's thrilling!

Richard I mean it. You're so alive and vital and

different from other people.

Sorel   I'm so frightened that you'll be bored here.

Richard   Bored! Why should I be?

Sorel   Oh, I don't know. But you won't be, will you? – or
if you are, tell me at once, and we'll do something quite
different.

Richard   You're rather a dear, you know.

Sorel   I'm not. (*Rises and goes C.*) I'm devastating, entirely
lacking in restraint. So's Simon. It's Father's and Mother's
fault, really; you see, they're so vague – they've spent their
lives cultivating their Arts and not devoting any time to
ordinary conventions and manners and things. I'm the only
one who sees that, so I'm trying to be better. I'd love to be
beautifully poised and carry off difficult situations with a lift
of the eyebrows—

Richard   I'm sure you could carry off anything.

Sorel (*moves to R. corner of sofa*)   There you are, you see,
saying the right thing! You *always* say the right thing, and
no one knows a bit what you're really thinking. That's what
I adore.

Richard   I'm afraid to say anything now, in case you
think I'm only being correct.

Sorel   But you are correct. I wish you'd teach Simon to
be correct too. (*Sits beside* **Richard** *again.*)

Richard   It would be uphill work, I'm afraid.

Sorel   Why, don't you like him?

Richard   I've only met him for a moment.

There is an uncomfortable pause.

Sorel   Would you like to see the garden?

Richard (*he half rises*)   Very much indeed.

Sorel   No, as a matter of fact (**Richard** *sits again.*) we'd better wait until after tea. (*Another pause.*) Shall I sing you something?

Richard   Please – I should love it.

They both rise. **Sorel** *goes reluctantly to piano.*

Sorel (*comes slowly to sofa*)   I don't want to really a bit – only I'm trying to entertain you. It's as easy as pie to talk in someone else's house, like at the dance the other night, but here on my own *ground* I'm finding it difficult.

Richard (*puzzled*)   I'm sorry.

Sorel   Oh, it isn't your fault; honestly, it isn't – you're awfully kind and responsive. (*Sits on sofa.*) What shall we do?

Richard   I'm quite happy talking (*Sits beside her.*) to you.

Pause.

Sorel   Can you play Mah Jong?

Richard   No, I'm afraid I can't.

Sorel   I'm *so* glad – I *do* hate it so.

Clara *enters, with a small stool for tea, and places it with a bang at* **Richard**'s *feet.*

Sorel   Here's tea!

Clara   Where's your mother, dear?

Sorel   Out in the garden, I think.

Clara   It's starting to rain. (*Goes out L. and fetches tea-tray loaded with tea-things, which she puts on stool.*)

Sorel   Oh, everyone will come dashing in, then. How awful!

Richard (*rises and goes C.*)   Won't the luggage get rather wet out there?

Sorel   What luggage?

Clara   I'll bring it in when I've made the tea.

Richard (*goes out R. and returns with two suitcases, which he places down R.C.*)   Oh, don't trouble; I'll do it now.

Sorel   We ought to have got William up from the village.

Clara   It's Saturday.

Sorel   I know it is.

Clara   He's playing cricket.

Sorel *rushes to help* **Richard**.

Sorel   Do sit down and smoke. I can easily manage it.

Richard   Certainly not.

Sorel (*goes out*)   How typical of Myra to have so many bags! . . . Ooh!

She staggers with a suitcase. **Richard** *goes to her assistance, and they both drop it.*

There now – we've probably broken something!

Richard   Well, it's not my bag, so it doesn't matter.

Richard *goes out to get the last case while* **Sorel** *holds the door open.*

Richard   This is the last one. . . . (*He brings in a dressing-case, and wipes his hand on his handkerchief.*)

Sorel   Do you know where to wash if you want to?

Richard   No – but I'm all right. (*They both stand leaning on piano, talking.*)

Re-enter **Clara** *with teapot. She puts it on stool and exits again.* **Simon** *and* **Myra** *come in from the garden.*

Myra (*goes to shake hands with* **Sorel**, *but* **Simon** *pulls her towards sofa*)   Hallo, Sorel! How are you?

Sorel   I'm splendid. Do you know Mr Greatham?

Myra   Oh, yes; we've met several times.

Simon   Come and sit down, Myra. (**Myra**, *pulled by*

Simon, *sits L. side of sofa,* **Simon** *R. side.*)

David *and* **Jackie** *come downstairs,* **David** *leading her by the elbow like a small child. They come C.*

David   Is tea ready?

Sorel   Yes; just.

David (*leaving* **Jackie** *R.C. and crossing to* **Simon**)   Simon, come and be nice to Miss Coryton.

Simon   We've met already.

David (*drags him out of his seat, and sits there himself*)   That's no reason for you not to be nice to her.

Myra (*firmly*)   How do you do?

David   How do you do? Are you staying here?

Myra   I hope so.

Simon *moves round to behind L. corner of sofa and sits on table.*

David   You must forgive me for being rather frowsy, but I've been working hard.

Sorel   Father, this is Mr Greatham.

Richard *takes a step down R.*

David   How are you? When did you arrive?

Richard   This afternoon.

David   Good. Have some tea. (*He begins to pour it out.*) Everyone had better put their own sugar and milk in, or we shall get muddled. Where's your mother, Simon?

Simon (*moves round and takes a cup of tea and a piece of cake, then returns to his seat*)   She was last seen in the punt.

David   How extraordinary! She can't punt.

Sorel   Sandy Tyrell's with her.

David   Oh, well, she'll be all right, then. (*A slight pause.*) Who is he?

Sorel I don't know.

David Do sit down, everybody.

Jackie sits on form below piano. Enter **Judith** *and* **Sandy** *from the garden. She comes to C. and kicks off galoshes.*

Judith There's going to be a thunderstorm. I felt sick this morning. This is Sandy Tyrell – everybody—

Sorel Mother, I want you to meet Mr Greatham.

Richard *goes to her and shakes hands, then returns to piano.*

Judith Oh, yes. You were here before, weren't you?

Sorel Before *what*, darling?

Sorel *crosses and gets a cup of tea and returns with it to settee down R.*

Judith Before I went out in the punt. There was somebody else here, too – a fair girl. (*She sees* **Jackie**.) Oh, there you are! How do you do? Sit down, Sandy, and eat anything you want. Give Sandy some bread-and-butter, Simon.

Judith *crosses L. and helps herself to tea, then sits in chair down L.*

Richard *and* **Jackie** *sit on form below piano.* **Sandy** *remains standing C.*

Simon (*rises, picks up plate of bread-and-butter, crosses to* **Sandy** *and ungraciously thrusts it into his hands, then returns to his seat*) Here you are!

Sandy Thanks.

There is a long pause; then **Myra** *and* **Richard** *speak together.*

| **Richard** | | How far are you from Maidenhead, exactly? |
| **Myra** | (*together*) | What a pity it's raining – we might have had some tennis— |

They both stop, to let the other go on. There is another terrible silence.

Myra	⎫	I adore the shape of this hall – it's so—
	⎬ (*together*)	
Richard	⎭	The train was awfully crowded coming down—

They both stop again, and there is another dead silence, during which the curtain slowly falls.

Act Two

It is after dinner on the Saturday evening.

David *and* **Myra** *are seated on the settee down R.* **Sandy** *and* **Jackie** *are seated on form below piano.* **Sorel** *is standing down C. with her back to the audience.* **Simon** *is seated on R. arm of sofa.* **Richard** *is seated on sofa.* **Judith** *is seated in chair down L. Everyone is talking and arguing.*

The following scene should be played with great speed.

Simon Who'll go out?

Sorel I don't mind.

Simon No; you always guess it too quickly.

Jackie What do we have to do?

Judith Choose an adverb, and then—

Simon Someone goes out, you see, and comes in, and you've chosen a word among yourselves, and she or he, whoever it is, asks you some sort of question, and you have to—

Sorel (*moves up to* **Simon**) Not an ordinary question, Simon; they have to ask them to do something in the manner of the word, and then—

Simon Then, you see, you act whatever it is—

Sorel The answer to the question, you see?

Richard (*apprehensively*) What sort of thing is one expected to do?

Judith Quite usual things, like reciting 'If', or playing the piano—

Richard I can't play the piano.

Simon Never mind; you can fake it, as long as it conveys an idea of the word.

Jackie   The word we've all thought of?

Sorel (*impatient*)   Yes, the word we've chosen when whoever it is is out of the room.

Jackie   I'm afraid I don't quite understand yet.

Simon   Never mind; I'll explain. You see, someone goes out. . . .

Sorel   I'll go out the first time, just to show her.

Judith   It's quite simple – all you have to do is just act in the manner of the word.

Sorel   Look here, everybody, I'm going out.

Simon   All right; go on.

Sorel *moves to door down L. but stops in doorway as* **Myra** *speaks.*

Myra   The History game's awfully good – when two people go out, and come back as Mary Queen of Scots and Crippen or somebody.

Sandy (*despondently*)   I'm no earthly good at this sort of thing.

Sorel   I'll show you, Sandy. You see . . .

Judith   There's always 'How, When, and Where?' We haven't played that for ages.

Simon   We will afterwards. We'll do this one first. Go on, Sorel.

Sorel   Don't be too long. (*She goes out door down L.*)

Simon (*rises and faces company*)   Now then.

Judith   'Bitterly'.

Simon   No, we did that last week; she'll know.

David   'Intensely'.

Judith   Too difficult.

Richard   There was an amusing game I played once at the Harringtons' house. Everyone was blindfolded except—

Simon   (*goes back to corner of sofa*)   This room's not big enough for that. What about 'winsomely'?

Jackie   I wish I knew what we had to do.

Judith   You'll see when we start playing.

Myra   (*rises and crosses to table behind sofa, takes cigarette and lights it*)   If we start playing.

Simon   Mother's brilliant at this. Do you remember when we played it at the Mackenzies'?

Judith   Yes, and Blanche was so cross when I kissed Freddie's ear in the manner of the word.

Richard   What was the word?

Judith   I can't remember.

Myra   (*having lit cigarette she returns to her seat*)   Perhaps it's as well.

David   What about 'drearily'?

Judith   Not definite enough.

Simon   'Winsomely' is the best.

Judith   She's sure to guess it straight off.

Sandy   (*confidentially to* **Jackie**)   These games are much too brainy for me.

David   Young Norman Robertson used to be marvellous – do you remember?

Simon   Yes, wonderful sense of humour.

Myra   He's lost it all since his marriage.

Judith   I didn't know you knew him.

Myra   Well, considering he married my cousin—

Pause.

Richard   We don't seem to be getting on with the game.

Judith   We haven't thought of a word yet.

Myra   'Brightly'.

Simon   Too obvious.

Myra   Very well – don't snap at me!

Judith   'Saucily'. I've got a lovely idea for 'saucily'.

Myra (*to* **Simon**)   I should think 'rudely' would be the easiest.

Simon   Don't be sour, Myra.

Judith   The great thing is to get an obscure word.

Simon   What a pity Irene isn't here – she knows masses of obscure words.

Myra   She's probably picked them up from her obscure friends.

Simon   It's no use being catty about Irene; she's a perfect darling.

Myra   I wasn't being catty at all.

Simon   Yes, you were.

Sorel (*off*)   Hurry up!

Judith   Quickly, now! We must think—

Jackie (*rises and comes C. – helpfully*)   'Appendicitis'.

Judith (*witheringly*)   That's not an adverb.

Simon   You're thinking of Charades.

Jackie *returns to her seat.*

Sandy   Charades are damned good fun.

Simon   Yes, but we don't happen to be doing them at the moment.

Sandy   Sorry.

Judith   'Saucily'.

Simon   No, 'winsomely' is better.

Judith   All right. Call her in.

Simon (*calling*)   Sorel – come on; we're ready.

Sandy (*hoarsely to* **Simon**)   Which is it – 'saucily' or 'winsomely'?

Simon (*whispering*)   'Winsomely'.

Re-enter **Sorel**. *She moves to C.*

Sorel (*to* **Judith**)   Go and take a flower out of that vase and give it to Richard.

Judith   Very well.

She trips lightly over to the vase on the piano, gurgling with coy laughter, selects a flower, then goes over to **Richard**; *pursing her lips into a mock smile, she gives him the flower with a little girlish gasp at her own daring and wags her finger archly at him, and returns to her seat.* **Richard** *puts flower on sofa table and sits again.*

Simon   Marvellous, Mother!

Sorel (*laughing*)   Oh, lovely! (*Looking round the company.*) Now, Myra, get up and say good-bye to everyone in the manner of the word.

Myra (*rises and starts with* **David**)   Good-bye. It really has been most delightful—

Judith   No, no, no!

Myra (*moves C.*)   Why – what do you mean?

Judith   You haven't got the right intonation a bit.

Simon   Oh, Mother darling, do shut up!

Myra (*acidly*)   Remember what an advantage you have over we poor amateurs, Judith, having been a professional for so long. (*Returns to her seat.*)

Judith I don't like 'so long' very much.

Sorel Do you think we might go on now?

Myra Go to the next one; I'm not going to do any more.

Simon Oh, please do. You were simply splendid.

Sorel It doesn't matter. (*To* **Richard**.) Light a cigarette in the manner of the word. (**Richard** *rises*.)

Richard (*takes cigarette from box on sofa table*) I've forgotten what it is.

Judith (*grimacing at him violently*) You remember . . .

Richard Oh, yes.

He goes to **Sorel** *C. and proceeds to light a cigarette with great abandon, winking his eye and chucking* **Sorel** *under the chin, then looks round panic-stricken.*

Judith Oh, no, no, no!

Myra I can't think *what* that's meant to be.

Richard (*offended*) I was doing my best.

Judith It's so *frightfully* easy, and nobody can do it right.

Simon I believe you've muddled it up.

Richard (*returns to his seat*) You'd better go on to the next one.

Judith Which word were you doing? Whisper—

Richard (*leans over to her, whispering*) 'Saucily'.

Judith I knew it! – he was doing the wrong word. (*She whispers to him.*)

Richard Oh, I see. I'm so sorry.

Judith Give him another chance.

Simon No, it's Jackie's turn now; it will come round to him again, I'm afraid.

Sorel (*moves to* **Jackie**) Do a dance in the manner of the word.

Jackie (*giggling*)   I can't.

Judith   Nonsense! Of course you can.

Jackie   I can't – honestly – I . . .

Simon (*crosses and pulls her to her feet*)   Go on; have a shot at it.

Jackie   No, I'd much rather not. Count me out.

Judith   Really, the ridiculous fuss everyone makes—

Jackie   I'm awfully stupid, at anything like this.

Sorel   It's only a game, after all.

David   Come along – try.

Jackie (*dragging back*)   I couldn't – please don't ask me to. I simply couldn't. (*She sits again.*)

Simon   Leave her alone if she doesn't want to.

Sorel (*irritably*)   What's the use of playing at all, if people won't do it properly!

Judith   It's *so* simple.

Sandy   It's awfully difficult if you haven't done it before.

Simon   Go on to the next one.

Sorel (*firmly*)   Unless everyone's in it we won't play at all.

Simon   Now, don't lose your temper.

Sorel   Lose my temper! I like that! No one's given me the slightest indication of what the word is – you all argue and squabble—

David   Talk, talk, talk! Everybody talks too much.

Judith   It's so surprising to me when people won't play up. After all—

Jackie (*with spirit*)   It's a hateful game, anyhow, and I don't want to play it again ever.

Sorel   You haven't played it at all yet.

Simon   Don't be rude, Sorel.

Sorel   Really, Simon, the way you go on is infuriating!

Simon   It's always the same; whenever Sorel goes out she gets quarrelsome.

Sorel   Quarrelsome!

Simon (*patting her hand in a fatherly fashion*)   Don't worry, Jackie; you needn't do anything you don't want to.

Judith   I think, for the future, we'd better confine our efforts to social conversation and not attempt anything in the least intelligent.

Simon   How can you be so unkind, Mother!

Judith (*sharply*)   Don't speak to me like that!

Jackie (*speaking winsomely*)   It's all my fault – I know I'm awfully silly, but it embarrasses me so terribly doing anything in front of people.

Sorel (*with acidity*)   I should think the word was 'winsomely'.

Simon   You must have been listening outside the door, then.

Sorel   Not at all – Miss Coryton gave it away.

Simon   Why 'Miss Coryton' all of a sudden? You've been calling her Jackie all the evening. You're far too grand, Sorel.

Sorel (*stamping her foot*)   And you're absolutely maddening – I'll never play another game with you as long as I live!

Simon   That won't break my heart.

Judith   Stop, stop, stop!

Simon (*grabbing **Jackie**'s hand – he pulls her up to window*) Come out in the garden. I'm sick of this.

Sorel (*following them up and shouting after them*)   Don't let him take you on the river; he isn't very good at it.

Simon (*over his shoulder*)   Ha, ha! – very funny!

He drags **Jackie** *off.* **Sorel** *returns to C.*

Judith   Sorel, you're behaving disgracefully.

Sorel   Simon ought to go into the army, or something.

David   You both ought to be in reformatories.

Sorel   This always happens whenever we play a game. We're a beastly family, and I hate us.

Judith   Speak for yourself, dear.

Sorel   I can't, without speaking for everyone else too – we're all exactly the same, and I'm ashamed of us. (*Grasps* **Sandy**'s *hand and drags him off door L.*) Come into the library, Sandy.

Myra (*rises and goes to table behind sofa*)   Charming! It's all perfectly charming!

David (*rising and standing R.C.*)   I think it would be better, Judith, if you exercised a little more influence over the children.

Judith   That's right – blame it all on me.

David   After all, dear, you started it, by snapping everybody up.

Judith (*rises and crosses to him*)   You ought never to have married me, David; it was a great mistake.

David   The atmosphere of this house is becoming more unbearable every day, and all because Simon and Sorel are allowed to do exactly what they like.

Judith   You sit upstairs all day, writing your novels.

David   Novels which earn us our daily bread.

Judith   'Daily bread' – nonsense! (*Crosses down R.*) We've got enough money to keep us in comfort until we die.

David   That will be very soon, if we can't get a little peace. (*To* **Myra**.) Come out into the garden—

They both go up to window.

Judith   I sincerely hope the night air will cool you.

David (*coming down to* **Judith**)   I don't know what's happened to you, lately, Judith.

Judith   Nothing's happened to me – nothing ever does. You're far too smug to allow it.

David   Smug! Thank you.

Judith   Yes, smug, smug, smug! And pompous!

David   I hope you haven't been drinking, dear?

Judith   Drinking! (*Laughs.*) Huh! that's very amusing!

David   I think it's rather tragic, at your time of life.

He goes out with **Myra**.

Judith *goes after them as if to speak, changes her mind, and comes down to L. corner of sofa.*

Judith   David's been a good husband to me, but he's wearing a bit thin now.

Richard (*rises*)   Would you like me to go? To leave you alone for a little?

Judith   Why? Are you afraid I shall become violent?

Richard (*smiling*)   No; I merely thought perhaps I was in the way.

Judith   I hope you're not embarrassed – I couldn't bear you to be embarrassed.

Richard   Not in the least.

Judith   Marriage is a hideous affair altogether, don't you think?

Richard   I'm really hardly qualified to judge, you see—

Judith   Do stop being non-committal, just for once; it's doubly annoying in the face of us all having lost control so lamentably.

Richard   I'm sorry.

Judith   There's nothing to be sorry for, really, because, after all, it's your particular 'thing', isn't it? – observing everything and not giving yourself away an inch.

Richard   I suppose it is.

Judith   You'll get used to us in time, and then you'll feel cosier. Why don't you sit down? (*She sits on sofa.*)

Richard (*sits beside her*)   I'm enjoying myself very much.

Judith   It's very sweet of you to say so, but I don't see how you can be.

Richard (*laughing suddenly*)   But I am!

Judith   There now, that was quite a genuine laugh! We're getting on. Are you in love with Sorel?

Richard (*surprised and embarrassed*)   In love with Sorel?

Judith (*repentantly*)   Now I've killed it – I've murdered the little tender feeling of comfort that was stealing over you, by sheer tactlessness! Will you teach me to be tactful?

Richard   Did you really think I was in love with Sorel?

Judith   It's so difficult to tell, isn't it? – I mean, you might not know yourself. She's very attractive.

Richard   Yes, she is – very.

Judith   Have you heard her sing?

Richard   No, not yet.

Judith   She sings beautifully. Are you susceptible to music?

Richard   I'm afraid I don't know very much about it.

Judith   You probably are, then. I'll sing you something.

Richard Please do.

Judith (*rises and crosses to piano; he rises and stands C.*) It's awfully sad for a woman of my temperament to have a grown-up daughter, you know. I have to put my pride in my pocket and develop in her all the charming little feminine tricks which will eventually cut me out altogether.

Richard That wouldn't be possible.

Judith I do hope you meant that, because it was a sweet remark. (*She is at the piano, turning over music.*)

Richard (*crosses to piano*) Of course I meant it.

Judith Will you lean on the piano in an attentive attitude? It's such a help.

Richard (*leaning on piano*) You're an extraordinary person.

Judith (*beginning to play*) In what way extraordinary?

Richard When I first met Sorel, I guessed what you'd be like.

Judith Did you, now? And am I?

Richard (*smiling*) Exactly.

Judith Oh, well! . . . (*She plays and sings a little French song.*)

There is a slight pause when it is finished.

Richard (*with feeling*) Thank you.

Judith (*rising from the piano*) It's pretty, isn't it?

Richard Perfectly enchanting.

Judith (*crosses to sofa*) Shall we sit down again? (*She re-seats herself on sofa.*)

Richard (*moving over to her*) Won't you sing any more?

Judith No, no more – I want you to talk to me and tell me all about yourself, and the things you've done.

Richard (*sits beside her*) I've done nothing.

Judith   What a shame! Why not?

Richard   I never realize how *dead* I am until I meet people like you. It's depressing, you know.

Judith   What nonsense! You're not a bit dead.

Richard   Do you always live here?

Judith   I'm going to, from now onwards. I intend to sink into a very beautiful old age. When the children marry, I shall wear a cap.

Richard (*smiling*)   How absurd!

Judith   I don't mean a funny cap.

Richard   You're far too full of vitality to sink into anything.

Judith   It's entirely spurious vitality. If you troubled to look below the surface, you'd find a very wistful and weary spirit. I've been battling with life for a long time.

Richard   Surely such successful battles as yours have been are not wearying?

Judith   Yes, they are – frightfully. I've reached an age now when I just want to sit back and let things go on around me – and they do.

Richard   I should like to know exactly what you're thinking about – really.

Judith   I was thinking of calling you Richard. It's such a nice uncompromising name.

Richard   I should be very flattered if you would.

Judith   I won't suggest you calling me Judith until you feel really comfortable about me.

Richard   But I do – Judith.

Judith   I'm awfully glad. Will you give me a cigarette?

Richard (*producing case*)   Certainly.

Judith (*taking one*)   Oh, what a divine case!

Richard   It was given to me in Japan three years ago. All those little designs mean things.

Judith (*bending over it*)   What sort of things?

He lights her cigarette.

Richard   Charms for happiness, luck, and – love.

Judith   Which is the charm for love?

Richard   That one.

Judith   What a dear!

Richard *kisses her gently on the neck.*

Judith (*she sits upright, with a scream*)   Richard!

Richard (*stammering*)   I'm afraid I couldn't help it.

Judith (*dramatically*)   What are we to do? What are we to do?

Richard   I don't know.

Judith (*rises, thrusts the case in his hand and crosses to R.C.*)   David must be told – everything!

Richard (*alarmed*)   Everything?

Judith (*enjoying herself*)   Yes, yes. There come moments in life when it is necessary to be honest – absolutely honest. I've trained myself always to shun the underhand methods other women so often employ – the truth must be faced fair and square—

Richard (*extremely alarmed*)   The truth? I don't quite understand. (*He rises.*)

Judith   Dear Richard, you want to spare me, I know – you're so chivalrous; but it's no use. After all, as I said before, David has been a good husband to me, according to his lights. This may, of course, break him up rather, but it can't be helped. I wonder – oh, I wonder how he'll take it! They say suffering's good for writers, it strengthens their psychology. Oh, my poor, poor David! Never mind. You'd better go out into the garden and wait—

Richard (*flustered*)   Wait? What for? (*Moves to C.*)

Judith   For me, Richard, for me. I will come to you later. Wait in the summer-house. I had begun to think that Romance was dead, that I should never know it again. Before, of course, I had my work and my life in the theatre, but now, nothing – nothing! Everything is empty and hollow, like a broken shell. (*She sinks on to form below piano, and looks up at* **Richard** *with a tragic smile, then looks quickly away.*)

Richard   Look here, Judith, I apologize for what I did just now. I—

Judith (*ignoring all interruption, she rises and crosses to L.C.*)   But now you have come, and it's all changed – it's magic! I'm under a spell that I never thought to recapture again. Go along—

She pushes him towards the garden.

Richard (*protesting*)   But, Judith—

Judith (*pushing him firmly until he is off*)   Don't – don't make it any harder for me. I am quite resolved – and it's the only possible way. Go, go!

She pushes him into the garden and waves to him bravely with her handkerchief; then she comes back into the room and powders her nose before the glass and pats her hair into place. Then, assuming an expression of restrained tragedy, she opens the library door, screams and recoils genuinely shocked to C.

After a moment or two, **Sorel** *and* **Sandy** *come out rather sheepishly and stand L.C.*

Sorel   Look here, Mother, I—

Judith   Sorel, what am I to say to you?

Sorel   I don't know, Mother.

Judith   Neither do I.

Sandy It was my fault, Mrs Bliss – Judith—

Judith What a fool I've been! What a blind fool!

Sorel Mother, are you *really* upset?

Judith (*with feeling*) I'm stunned!

Sorel But, darling—

Judith (*gently*) Don't speak for a moment, Sorel; we must all be very quiet, and think—

Sorel It was nothing, really. For Heaven's sake—

Judith Nothing! I open the library door casually, and what do I see? I ask you, what do I see?

Sandy I'm most awfully sorry. . . .

Judith Ssshh! It has gone beyond superficial apologies.

Sorel Mother, be natural for a minute.

Judith I don't know what you mean, Sorel. I'm trying to realize a very bitter truth as calmly as I can.

Sorel There's nothing so very bitter about it.

Judith My poor child!

Sorel (*suddenly*) Very well, then! I love Sandy, and he loves me!

Judith That is the only possible excuse for your behaviour.

Sorel Why shouldn't we love each other if we want to?

Judith Sandy was in love with me this afternoon.

Sorel Not real love – you know it wasn't.

Judith (*bitterly*) I know now.

Sandy (*crosses to L. of* **Judith**) I say – look here – I'm most awfully sorry.

Judith There's nothing to be sorry for, really; it's my fault for having been so – so ridiculous.

Sorel   Mother!

Judith (*sadly*)   Yes, ridiculous. (*Goes up to piano.*) I'm getting old, old, and the sooner I face it the better. (*She picks up mirror, looks at herself, and puts it down again quickly.*)

Sorel (*hopelessly*)   But, darling . . .

Judith (*splendidly – she goes to* **Sorel**)   Youth will be served. You're so pretty, Sorel, far prettier than I ever was – I'm very glad you're pretty.

Sandy (*moving down R.*)   I feel a fearful cad.

Judith   Why should you? You've answered the only call that really counts – the call of Love, and Romance, and Spring. I forgive you, Sandy, completely. There! (*She goes to him and pats his shoulder.*)

Sorel   Well, that's all right then. (*She sits on sofa.*)

Judith   I resent your tone, Sorel; you seem to be taking things too much for granted. Perhaps you don't realize that I am making a great sacrifice. (*Pointing to* **Sandy**.)

Sorel   Sorry, darling.

Judith (*starting to act*)   It's far from easy, at my time of life, to—

Sorel (*playing up*)   Mother – Mother, say you understand and forgive!

Judith   Understand! You forget, dear, I am a woman.

Sorel   I know you are, Mother. That's what makes it all so poignant.

Judith (*magnanimously, to* **Sandy**)   If you want Sorel, truly, I give her to you – unconditionally.

Sandy (*dazed*)   Thanks – awfully, Mrs Bliss.

Judith   You can still call me Judith, can't you? – it's not much to ask.

Sandy   Judith!

Judith (*bravely*)   There, now. Away with melancholy. This is all tremendously exciting, and we must all be very happy.

Sorel   Don't tell Father – yet.

Judith   We won't tell anybody; it shall be *our* little secret.

Sorel   You are splendid, Mother!

Judith   Nonsense! I just believe in being honest with myself – it's awfully good for one, you know, so cleansing. I'm going upstairs now to have a little aspirin— (*She goes upstairs, and turns.*) Ah, Youth, Youth, what a strange, mad muddle you make of things! (*She goes off upstairs.*)

Sorel *heaves a slight sigh.*

Sorel   Well, that's that!

Sandy   Yes. (*Sits on form below piano, looking very gloomy.*)

Sorel   It's all right. Don't look so gloomy – I know you don't love me really.

Sandy (*startled*)   I say, Sorel—

Sorel   Don't protest; you know you don't – any more than I love you.

Sandy   But you told Judith—

Sorel (*nonchalantly*)   I was only playing up – one always plays up to Mother in this house; it's a sort of unwritten law.

Sandy   Didn't she mean all she said?

Sorel   No, not really; we none of us ever mean *anything*.

Sandy   She seemed awfully upset.

Sorel   It must have been a slight shock for her to discover us clasped tightly in each other's arms.

Sandy (*rising and moving to C.*)   I believe I do love you, Sorel.

Sorel   A month ago I should have let you go on believing that, but now I can't – I'm bent on improving myself.

Sandy   I don't understand.

Sorel   Never mind – it doesn't matter. You just fell a victim to the atmosphere, that's all. There we were alone in the library, with the windows wide open, and probably a nightingale somewhere about—

Sandy   I only heard a cuckoo.

Sorel   Even a cuckoo has charm, in moderation. (*Rises and goes to him.*) You kissed me because you were awfully nice and I was awfully nice and we both liked kissing very much. It was inevitable. Then Mother found us and got dramatic – her sense of the theatre is always fatal. She knows we shan't marry, the same as you and I do. You're under absolutely no obligation to me at all.

Sandy   I wish I understood you a bit better.

Sorel   Never mind about understanding me – let's go back into the library.

Sandy   All right.

They go off door down L.

After a moment's pause, **David** *and* **Myra** *enter from the garden.*

David   . . . and, you see, he comes in and finds her there waiting for him.

They come down C.

Myra   She hadn't been away at all?

David   No; and that's psychologically right, I'm sure. No woman, under those circumstances, *would.*

Myra (*sitting on L. end of sofa*)   It's brilliant of you to see that. I do think the whole things sounds most excellent.

David   I got badly stuck in the middle of the book, when the boy comes down from Oxford – but it worked out all right eventually.

Myra   When shall I be able to read it?

David   I'll send you the proofs – you can help me correct them.

Myra   How divine! I shall feel most important.

David   Would you like a cigarette, or anything?

Myra   No, thank you.

David   I think I'll have a drink. (*He goes to table up by window, and pours out some plain soda-water.*)

Myra   Very well; give me some plain soda-water, then.

David   There isn't any ice – d'you mind?

Myra   Not a bit.

David (*bringing her drink*)   Here you are. (*He goes back and pours himself a whisky-and-soda, and returns to sofa.*)

Myra   Thank you. (*She sips it.*) I wonder where everybody is.

David   Not here, thank God.

Myra   It must be dreadfully worrying for you, having a houseful of people.

David (*sits down by her side*)   It depends on the people.

Myra   I have a slight confession to make.

David   Confession?

Myra   Yes. Do you know why I came down here?

David   Not in the least. I suppose one of us asked you, didn't they?

Myra   Oh, yes, they asked me, but—

David   Well?

Myra   I was invited once before – last September.

David   I was in America then.

Myra   Exactly.

David   How do you mean 'exactly'?

Myra   I didn't come. I'm a very determined woman, you know, and I made up my mind to meet you ages ago.

David   That was charming of you. I'm not much to meet really.

Myra   You see, I'd read *Broken Reeds*.

David   Did you like it?

Myra   Like it! I think it's one of the finest novels I've ever read.

David   There now!

Myra   How do you manage to know so much about women?

David   I'm afraid my knowledge of them is sadly superficial.

Myra   Oh, no; you can't call Evelyn's character superficial – it's amazing.

David   Why are you being so nice to me? Have you got a plan about something?

Myra (*laughing*)   How suspicious you are!

David   I can't help it – you're very attractive, and I'm always suspicious of attractive people, on principle.

Myra   Not a very good principle.

David (*leaning towards her*)   I'll tell you something – strictly between ourselves.

Myra   Do!

David   You're wrong about me.

Myra   Wrong? In what way?

David   I write very bad novels.

Myra   Don't be so ridiculous!

David   And you *know* I do, because you're an intelligent person.

Myra   I don't know anything of the sort.

David   Tell me why you're being nice to me.

Myra   Because I want to be.

David   Why?

Myra   You're a very clever and amusing man.

David   Splendid!

Myra   And I think I've rather lost my heart to you.

David   Shall we elope?

Myra   David!

David   There now, you've called me David!

Myra   Do you mind?

David   Not at all.

Myra   I'm not sure that you're being very kind.

David   What makes you think that?

Myra   You being rather the cynical author laughing up his sleeve at a gushing admirer.

David   I think you're a very interesting woman, and extremely nice-looking.

Myra   Do you?

David   Yes. Would you like me to make love to you?

Myra   (*rising*)   Really – I wish you wouldn't say things like that.

David   I've knocked you off your plate – I'll look away for a minute while you climb on to it again. (*He does so.*)

Myra   (*laughing affectedly. She puts her glass down on table*)   This is wonderful! (*She sits down again.*)

David (*turning*)   That's right. Now then—

Myra   Now then, what?

David (*leaning very close to her*)   You're adorable – you're magnificent – you're tawny—

Myra   I'm not tawny.

David   Don't argue.

Myra   This is sheer affectation.

David   Affectation's very nice.

Myra   No, it isn't – it's odious.

David   You mustn't get cross.

Myra   I'm not in the least cross.

David   Yes, you are – but you're very alluring.

Myra (*perking up*)   Alluring?

David   Terribly.

Myra   I can hear your brain clicking – it's very funny.

David   That was rather rude.

Myra   You've been consistently rude to me for hours.

David   Never mind.

Myra   Why have you?

David   I'm always rude to people I like.

Myra   Do you like me?

David   Enormously.

Myra   How sweet of you!

David   But I don't like your methods.

Myra   Methods? What methods?

David   You're far too pleasant to occupy yourself with the commonplace.

Myra   And you spoil yourself by trying to be clever.

David   Thank you.

Myra   Anyhow, I don't know what you mean by commonplace.

David   You mean you want me to explain?

Myra   Not at all.

David   Very well; I will.

Myra   I shan't listen. (*She stops up her ears.*)

David   You'll pretend not to, but you'll hear every word really.

Myra (*sarcastically*)   You're so inscrutable and quizzical – just what a feminine psychologist should be.

David   Yes, aren't I?

Myra   You frighten me dreadfully.

David   Darling!

Myra   Don't call me darling.

David   That's unreasonable. You've been trying to make me – all the evening.

Myra   Your conceit is outrageous!

David   It's not conceit at all. You've been firmly buttering me up because you want a nice little intrigue.

Myra (*rising*)   How dare you!

David (*pulling her down again*)   It's true, it's true. If it weren't, you wouldn't be so angry.

Myra   I think you're insufferable!

David (*taking her hand*)   Myra – dear Myra—

Myra (*snatching it away – she rises*)   Don't touch me!

David Let's have that nice little intrigue. (*He rises.*) The only reason I've been so annoying is that I love to see things as they are first, and then pretend they're what they're not.

Myra Words. (*Moves over R.*) Masses and masses of words!

David (*following her*) They're great fun to play with.

Myra I'm glad you think so. Personally, they bore me stiff.

David (*catching her right hand again*) Myra – don't be statuesque.

Myra Let go my hand!

David You're charming.

Myra (*furiously*) Let go my hand!

David I won't!

Myra You will!

She slaps his face hard, and he seizes her in his arms and kisses her.

David (*between kisses*) You're – perfectly – sweet.

Myra (*giving in*) David!

David You must say it's an entrancing amusement. (*He kisses her again.*)

Judith *appears at the top of the stairs and sees them. They break away, he still keeping hold of her hand.*

Judith (*coming down C.*) Forgive me for interrupting.

David Are there any chocolates in the house?

Judith No, David.

David I should like a chocolate more than anything in the world, at the moment.

Judith This is a very unpleasant situation, David.

David (*agreeably*) Horrible!

Judith   We'd better talk it all over.

Myra (*making a movement*)   I shall do nothing of the sort!

Judith   Please – please don't be difficult.

David   I apologize, Judith.

Judith   Don't apologize – I quite understand.

Myra   Please let go of my hand, David; I should like to go to bed.

She pulls her hand away.

Judith   I should stay if I were you – it would be more dignified.

David (*moves a step towards* **Judith**)   There isn't any real necessity for a scene.

Judith   I don't want a scene. I just want to straighten things out.

David   Very well – go ahead.

Judith   June has always been an unlucky month for me.

Myra   Look here, Judith – I'd like to explain one thing—

Judith (*austerely*)   I don't wish to hear any explanations or excuses – they're so cheapening. This was bound to happen sooner or later – it always does, to everybody. The only thing is to keep calm.

David   I am – perfectly.

Judith (*sharply*)   There is such a thing as being too calm.

David   Sorry, dear.

Judith   Life has dealt me another blow, but I don't mind.

David   What did you say?

Judith (*crossly*)   I said Life had dealt me another blow, but I didn't mind.

David   Rubbish!

Judith (*gently*) You're probably irritable, dear, because you're in the wrong. It's quite usual.

David Now, Judith—

Judith Ssshhh! Let me speak – it is my right.

Myra I don't see why.

Judith (*surprised*) I am the injured party, am I not?

Myra Injured?

Judith (*firmly*) Yes, extremely injured.

David (*contemptuously*) Injured!

Judith Your attitude, David, is nothing short of deplorable.

David It's all nonsense – sheer, unbridled nonsense!

Judith No, David, you can't evade the real issues as calmly as that. I've known for a long time – I've realized subconsciously for years that you've stopped caring for me in 'that way'.

David (*irritably*) What do you mean – 'that way'?

Judith (*with a wave of the hand*) Just that way. . . . It's rather tragic, but quite inevitable. I'm growing old now – men don't grow old like women, as you'll find to your cost, Myra, in a year or two. David has retained his youth astonishingly, perhaps because he has had fewer responsibilities and cares than I—

Myra This is all ridiculous hysteria.

David (*goes to* **Myra**) No, Myra – Judith is right. What are we to do?

Myra (*furious*) Do? Nothing!

Judith (*ignoring her*) Do you love her truly, David?

David (*looks* **Myra** *up and down as if to make sure*) Madly!

Myra (*astounded*) David!

David (*intensely*) You thought just now that I was joking. Couldn't you see that all my flippancy was only a mask, hiding my real emotions – crushing them down desperately—?

Myra (*scared*) But, David, I—

Judith I knew it! The time has come for the dividing of the ways.

Myra What on earth do you mean?

Judith I mean that I am not the sort of woman to hold a man against his will.

Myra You're both making a mountain out of a molehill. David doesn't love me madly, and I don't love him. It's—

Judith Ssshhh! – you *do* love him. I can see it in your eyes – in your every gesture. David, I give you to her – freely and without rancour. We must all be good friends, always.

David Judith, do you mean this?

Judith (*with a melting look*) You know I do.

David How can we ever repay you?

Judith Just by being happy. (*Sits on sofa.*) I may leave this house later on – I have a feeling that its associations may become painful, specially in the autumn—

Myra Look here, Judith—

Judith (*shouting her down*) October is such a mournful month in England. I think I shall probably go abroad – perhaps a *pension* somewhere in Italy, with cypresses in the garden. I've always loved cypresses, they are such sad, weary trees.

David (*goes to her, speaking in a broken voice*) What about the children?

Judith We must share them, dear.

David I'll pay you exactly half the royalties I receive from everything, Judith.

Judith (*bowing her head*)   That's very generous of you.

David   You have behaved magnificently. This is a crisis in our lives, and thanks to you—

Myra (*almost shrieking – moves over to* **Judith**, *but is stopped by* **David**)   Judith – I *will* speak – I—

David (*speaking in a very dramatic voice*)   Ssshhh, Myra darling – we owe it to Judith to keep control of our emotions – a scene would be agonizing for her now. She has been brave and absolutely splendid throughout. Let's not make things harder for her than we can help. Come, we'll go out into the garden.

Myra   I will *not* go out into the garden.

Judith (*twisting her handkerchief*)   Please go. (*Rises to L.C.*) I don't think I can bear any more just now.

David   So this is the end, Judith?

Judith   Yes, my dear – the end.

They shake hands sadly.

Simon *enters violently from the garden and breaks in between them.*

Simon   Mother – Mother, I've got something important to tell you.

Judith (*smiling bravely*)   Very well, dear.

Simon   Where's Sorel?

Judith   In the library, I'm afraid.

Simon (*runs to library door and shouts off*)   Sorel, come out – I've got something vital to tell you. (*Returns to C.*)

David (*fatherly*)   You seem excited, my boy! What has happened?

Sorel (*enters with* **Sandy** *and remains down L.*)   What's the matter?

Simon   I wish you wouldn't all look so depressed – it's good news!

David   Good news! I thought perhaps Jackie had been drowned—

Simon   No, Jackie hasn't been drowned – she's been something else.

Judith   Simon, what *do* you mean?

Simon (*running up C., calling off*)   Jackie – Jackie!

Jackie *enters coyly from the garden.* **Simon** *takes her hand and leads her down C.*

Simon   She has become engaged – to me!

Judith (*in heartfelt tones*)   Simon!

Sorel   Good heavens!

Judith   Simon, my dear! Oh, this is too much! (*She cries a little.*)

Simon   What on earth are you crying about, Mother?

Judith (*picturesquely*)   All my chicks leaving the nest! Now I shall only have my memories left. Jackie, come and kiss me.

Jackie *goes to her.*

Simon *goes to his* **Father**, *who congratulates him.*

Judith   You must promise to make my son happy—

Jackie (*worried*)   But, Mrs Bliss—

Judith   Ssshhh! I understand. I have not been a mother for nothing.

Jackie (*wildly*)   But it's not true – we don't—

Judith   You're trying to spare my feelings – I know—

Myra (*furiously*)   Well, I'm not going to spare your feelings, or anyone else's. You're the most infuriating set of hypocrites I've ever seen. This house is a complete featherbed of false emotions – you're posing, self-centred egotists, and I'm sick to death of you.

Simon Myra!

Myra Don't speak to me – I've been working up for this, only every time I opened my mouth I've been mowed down by theatrical effects. You haven't got one sincere or genuine feeling among the lot of you – you're artificial to the point of lunacy. It's a great pity you ever left the stage, Judith – it's your rightful home. You can rant and roar there as much as ever you like—

Judith Rant and roar! May God forgive you!

Myra And let me tell you this—

Simon (*interrupting*) I'm not going to allow you to say another word to Mother—

They all try to shout each other down.

Sorel		You ought to be ashamed of yourself—
Myra	(*together*)	Let me speak – I will speak—
David		Look here, Myra—
Judith		This is appalling – appalling!

Sorel		You must be stark, staring mad—
Myra	(*together*)	Never again – never as long as I live—
David		You don't seem to grasp one thing that—
Simon		Why are you behaving like this, anyhow?

In the middle of the pandemonium of everyone talking at once, **Richard** *comes in from the garden. He looks extremely apprehensive, imagining that the noise is the outcome of* **Judith**'s *hysterical* *confession of their lukewarm passion. He goes to* **Judith**'s *side, summoning all his diplomatic forces. As he speaks everyone stops talking.*

Richard (*with forced calm*)   What's happened? Is this a game?

Judith's *face gives a slight twitch; then, with a meaning look at* **Sorel** *and* **Simon**, *she answers him.*

Judith (*with spirit*)   Yes, and a game that must be played to the finish! (*She flings back her arm and knocks* **Richard** *up stage.*)

Simon (*grasping the situation*)   Zara! What does this mean? (*Advancing to her.*)

Judith (*in bell-like tones*)   So many illusions shattered – so many dreams trodden in the dust—

David (*collapsing on to the form in hysterics*)   *Love's Whirlwind*! Dear old *Love's Whirlwind*!

Sorel (*runs over to R., pushes* **Myra** *up stage and poses*)   I don't understand. You and Victor – My God!

Judith (*moves away L., listening*)   Hush! Isn't that little Pam crying—?

Simon (*savagely*)   She'll cry more, poor mite, when she realizes her mother is a – a—

Judith (*shrieking and turning to* **Simon**)   Don't say it! Don't say it!

Sorel   Spare her that.

Judith   I've given you all that makes life worth living – my youth, my womanhood, and now my child. Would you tear the very heart out of me? I tell you, it's infamous that men like you should be allowed to pollute Society. You have ruined my life. I have nothing left – nothing! God in heaven, where am I to turn for help? . . .

Sorel (*through clenched teeth – swings* **Simon** *round*)   Is this true? Answer me – is this true?

Judith (*wailing*)   Yes, yes!

Sorel (*as if to strike* **Simon**)   You cur!!!

Judith   Don't strike! He is your father!!!!

She totters and falls in a dead faint.

Myra, **Jackie**, **Richard** *and* **Sandy** *look on, dazed and aghast.*

Curtain.

Act Three

It is Sunday morning, about ten o'clock. There are various breakfast dishes on a side table L., and a big table is laid down L.C.

Sandy *appears at the top of the stairs. On seeing no one about, he comes down quickly and furtively helps himself to eggs and bacon and coffee, and seats himself at the table. He eats very hurriedly, casting occasional glances over his shoulder. A door bangs somewhere upstairs, which terrifies him; he chokes violently. When he has recovered he tears a bit of toast from a rack, butters it and marmalades it, and crams it into his mouth. Then, hearing somebody approaching, he darts into the library.*

Jackie *comes downstairs timorously; her expression is dismal, to say the least of it. She looks miserably out of the window at the pouring rain, then assuming an air of spurious bravado, she helps herself to some breakfast and sits down and looks at it. After one or two attempts to eat it, she bursts into tears.*

Sandy *opens the library door a crack, and peeps out.* **Jackie**, *seeing the door move, screams.* **Sandy** *re-enters.*

Jackie   Oh, it's only you – you frightened me!

Sandy   What's the matter?

Jackie *(sniffing)* Nothing.

Sandy   I say, don't cry. *(Sits down at the table, facing her.)*

Jackie   I'm not crying.

Sandy   You were – I heard you.

Jackie   It's this house. It gets on my nerves.

Sandy   I don't wonder – after last night.

Jackie   What were you doing in the library just now?

Sandy   Hiding.

Jackie   Hiding?

Sandy   Yes; I didn't want to run up against any of the family.

Jackie   I wish I'd never come. I had horrible nightmares with all those fearful dragons crawling across the walls.

Sandy   Dragons?

Jackie   Yes; I'm in a Japanese room – everything in it's Japanese, even the bed.

Sandy   How awful!

Jackie (*looks up at stairs to see if anyone is coming*)   I believe they're all mad, you know.

Sandy   The Blisses?

Jackie   Yes – they must be.

Sandy   I've been thinking that too.

Jackie   Do you suppose they know they're mad?

Sandy   No; people never do.

Jackie   It was Mr Bliss asked me down and he hasn't paid any attention to me at all. I went into his study soon after I arrived yesterday, and he said, 'Who the hell are you?'

Sandy   Didn't he remember?

Jackie   He did afterwards; then he brought me down to tea and left me.

Sandy   Are you really engaged to Simon?

Jackie (*bursting into tears again*)   Oh, no – I hope not!

Sandy   You were, last night.

Jackie   So were you – to Sorel.

Sandy   Not properly. We talked it over.

Jackie   I don't know what happened to me. I was in the garden with Simon, and he was being awfully sweet, and then he suddenly kissed me, and rushed into the house and said we were engaged – and that hateful Judith asked me to make him happy!

Sandy   That's exactly what happened to me and Sorel. Judith *gave* us to one another before we knew where we were.

Jackie   How frightful!

Sandy   I like Sorel, though; she was jolly decent about it afterwards.

Jackie   I think she's a cat.

Sandy   Why?

Jackie   Look at the way she lost her temper over that beastly game.

Sandy   All the same, she's better than the others.

Jackie   That wouldn't be very difficult.

Sandy (*hiccups loudly*)   Hic!

Jackie   I beg your pardon?

Sandy (*abashed*)   I say – I've got hiccups.

Jackie   Hold your breath.

Sandy   It was because I bolted my breakfast. (*He holds his breath.*)

Jackie   Hold it as long as you can.

Jackie *counts aloud. There is a pause.*

Sandy (*letting his breath go with a gasp*)   I can't any more – hic!

Jackie (*rises and gets sugar basin from side table down L.*)   Eat a lump of sugar.

Sandy (*taking one*)   I'm awfully sorry.

Jackie   I don't mind – but it's a horrid feeling, isn't it?

Sandy   Horrid – hic!

Jackie (*puts sugar basin down in front of* **Sandy** *and sits again – conversationally*)   People have died from hiccups you know.

Sandy (*gloomily*)   Have they?

Jackie   Yes. An aunt of mine once had them for three days without stopping.

Sandy   How beastly!

Jackie (*with relish*)   She had to have the doctor, and everything.

Sandy   I expect mine will *stop* soon.

Jackie   I hope they will.

Sandy   Hic! Damn!

Jackie   Drink some water the wrong way round.

Sandy   How do you mean – the wrong way round?

Jackie (*rising*)   The wrong side of the glass. I'll show you. (*She goes to side table L.*) There isn't any water.

Sandy (*rises and stands below table*)   Perhaps coffee would do as well.

Jackie   I've never tried coffee, but it might. (*Picks up his cup and hands it to him.*) There you are!

Sandy (*anxiously*)   What do I do?

Jackie   Tip it up and drink from the opposite side, sort of upside down.

Sandy (*trying*)   I can't reach any—

Jackie (*suddenly*)   Look out – somebody's coming. Bring it into the library – quick.

Sandy   Bring the sugar.

Jackie *picks up sugar basin and runs into library, leaving* **Sandy** *to follow.*

Sandy   I might need it again – hic! Oh, God!

He goes off into the library hurriedly.

Richard *comes downstairs. He glances round a trifle anxiously, goes to the window, looks out at the rain and shivers, then pulling himself together, he goes boldly to the barometer and taps it. It falls off the wall and breaks; he picks it up quickly and places it on the piano. Then he helps himself to some breakfast and sits down C. chair L. of table.*

Myra *appears on the stairs, very smart and bright.*

Myra (*vivaciously*)   Good morning.

Richard (*half rising*)   Good morning.

Myra   Are we the first down?

Richard   No, I don't think so.

Myra (*looking out of the window*)   Isn't this rain miserable?

Richard   Appalling! (*Starts to drink his coffee.*)

Myra   Where's the barometer? (*Crosses to side table L.*)

Richard (*at the mention of barometer,* **Richard** *chokes*)   On the piano.

Myra   What a queer place for it to be!

Richard   I tapped it, and it fell down.

Myra   Typical of this house. (*At side table.*) Are you having eggs and bacon, or haddock?

Richard   Haddock.

Myra   I'll have haddock too. I simply couldn't strike out a line for myself this morning. (*She helps herself to haddock and coffee, and sits down opposite* **Richard**.) Have you seen anybody.

Richard   No.

Myra   Good. We might have a little peace.

Richard   Have you ever stayed here before?

Myra   No, and I never will again.

Richard   I feel far from well this morning.

Myra   I'm so sorry, but not entirely surprised.

Richard   You see, I had the boiler room.

Myra   How terrible!

Richard   The window stuck and I couldn't open it – I was nearly suffocated. The pipes made peculiar noises all night, as well.

Myra (*looks round table*)   There isn't any sugar.

Richard   Oh – we'd better ring.

Myra   I doubt if it will be the slightest use, but we'll try.

Richard (*rising and ringing bell, above door L.*)   Do the whole family have breakfast in bed?

Myra   I neither know – nor care.

Richard (*returns to his seat*)   They're strange people, aren't they?

Myra   I think 'strange' is putting it mildly.

Enter **Clara**. *She comes to top of table.*

Clara   What's the matter?

Myra   There isn't any sugar.

Clara   There is – I put it 'ere myself.

Myra   Perhaps you'd find it for us, then?

Clara (*searching*)   That's very funny. I could 'ave sworn on me Bible oath I brought it in.

Myra   Well, it obviously isn't here now.

Clara   Someone's taken it – that's what it is.

Richard   It seems a queer thing to do.

Myra   Do you think you could get us some more?

Clara   Oh, yes, I'll fetch you some. (*Looks suspiciously and* *shakes her finger at* **Richard**.) But mark my words, there's been some 'anky-panky somewhere. (*She goes out.*)

Richard *looks after her.*

Myra   Clara is really more at home in a dressing-room than a house.

Richard   Was she Judith's dresser?

Myra   Of course. What other excuse could there possibly be for her?

Richard   She seems good-natured, but quaint.

Myra   This haddock's disgusting.

Richard   It isn't very nice, is it?

Re-enter **Clara**, *with sugar. She plumps it down on the table.*

Clara   There you are, dear!

Myra   Thank you.

Clara   It's a shame the weather's changed – you might 'ave 'ad such fun up the river.

There comes the sound of a crash from the library, and a scream.

What's that? (*Crosses to door and flings it open.*) Come out! What are you doing?

Jackie *and* **Sandy** *enter, rather shamefaced.*

Jackie   Good morning. I'm afraid we've broken a coffee-cup.

Clara   Was there any coffee in it?

Sandy   Yes, a good deal.

Clara (*rushing into the library*)   Oh dear, all over the carpet!

Sandy   It was my fault. I'm most awfully sorry.

Jackie *moves up L. above table.*

Clara *reappears.*

Clara   How did you come to do it?

Jackie   Well, you see, he had the hiccups, and I was showing him how to drink upside down.

Myra   How ridiculous!

Clara   Well, thank 'Eaven it wasn't one of the Crown Derbys.

She goes out.

Sandy   They've gone now, anyhow. (*Moves up to window and looks out.*)

Jackie   It was the sudden shock, I expect.

Sandy (*observantly*)   I say – it's raining!

Myra   It's been raining for hours.

Richard   Mrs Arundel—

Myra   Yes?

Richard   What are you going to do about – about to-day?

Myra   Nothing, except go up to London by the first train possible.

Richard   Do you mind if I come too? I don't think I could face another day like yesterday.

Jackie   Neither could I. (*Comes down to chair below* **Richard** *and sits.*)

Sandy (*comes eagerly to top of table and sits*)   Let's all go away – quietly!

Richard   Won't it seem a little rude if we *all* go?

Myra   Yes, it will. (*To* **Sandy**.) You and Miss Coryton must stay.

Jackie   I don't see why.

Sandy   I don't think they'd mind *very* much.

Myra   Yes, they would. You must let Mr Greatham and me get away first, anyhow. Ring for Clara. I want to find out about trains.

Sandy *rings bell and returns to his seat.*

Richard   I hope they won't all come down now.

Myra   You needn't worry about that; they're sure to roll about in bed for hours – they're such a slovenly family.

Richard   Have you got much packing to do?

Myra   No; I did most of it before I came down.

Re-enter **Clara** *– comes to top of table.*

Clara   What is it now?

Myra   Can you tell me what trains there are up to London?

Clara   When?

Myra   This morning.

Clara   Why? – you're not leaving, are you?

Myra   Yes; Mr Greatham and I have to be up by lunch-time.

Clara   Well, you've missed the 10.15.

Myra   Obviously.

Clara   There isn't another till 12.30.

Richard   Good heavens!

Clara   And that's a slow one.

She goes out.

Sandy (*to* **Jackie**)   Look here. I'll take you up in my car as soon as you like.

Jackie   All right; lovely!

Myra   Oh, you have got a car, haven't you?

Sandy   Yes.

Myra   Will it hold all of us?

Jackie   You said it would be rude for us all to go. Hadn't you and Mr Greatham better wait for the train?

Myra   Certainly not.

Richard (*to* **Sandy**)   If there is room, we should be very, very grateful.

Sandy   I think I can squeeze you in.

Myra   Then that's settled.

Jackie   When shall we start?

Sandy   As soon as you're ready. (*Rises.*)

Jackie   Mrs Arundel, what are you going to do about tipping Clara?

Myra   I don't know. (*To* **Richard**.) What do you think?

Richard   I've hardly seen her since I've been here.

Jackie   Isn't there a housemaid or anything?

Richard   I don't think so.

Sandy   Is ten bob enough?

Jackie   Each?

Myra   Too much.

Richard   We'd better give her one pound ten between us.

Myra   Very well, then. Will you do it, and we'll settle up in the car?

Richard   Must I?

Myra   Yes. Ring for her.

Richard   You'd do it much better.

Myra   Oh, no, I shouldn't. (*To* **Jackie**.) Come on; we'll finish our packing. (*Rises and goes, to stairs.*)

Jackie   All right. (*She follows* **Myra**.)

They begin to go upstairs.

Richard (*rises and goes to C.*)   Here – don't leave me.

Sandy (*crosses to door R.*)   I'll just go and look at the car. Will you all be ready in ten minutes?

Myra   Yes, ten minutes.

She goes off with **Jackie**.

Sandy   Righto! (*He rushes out.*)

Richard *moves over to bell as* **Clara** *re-enters with large tray.*

Clara   'Allo, where's everybody gone?

Richard (*sorts out thirty shillings from his note-case*)   They've gone to get ready. We're leaving in Mr Tyrell's car.

Clara   A bit sudden, isn't it?

Richard (*pressing the money into her hand*)   This is from all of us, Clara. Thank you very much for all your trouble.

Clara (*surprised*)   Aren't you a dear, now! There wasn't any trouble.

Richard   There must have been a lot of extra work.

Clara   One gets used to that 'ere.

Richard   Good morning, Clara.

Clara   Good morning, hope you've been comfortable.

Richard   Com— Oh, yes. (*He goes upstairs.*)

Clara *proceeds to clear away the dirty breakfast things, which she takes out singing* 'Tea for Two' *in a very shrill voice. She returns with a fresh pot of coffee, and meets* **Judith** *coming downstairs.*

Judith (*goes to head of table and sits*)   Good morning, Clara. Have the papers come?

Clara   Yes – I'll fetch them. (*She goes out and re-enters with papers, which she gives to* **Judith**.)

Judith   Thank you. You've forgotten my orange-juice.

Clara (*pours out a cup of coffee for* **Judith**)   No, I 'aven't, dear; it's just outside. (*She goes out again.*)

Judith *turns to the theatrical column of the 'Sunday Times'.*

Sorel *comes downstairs and kisses her.*

Sorel   Good morning, darling.

Judith   Listen to this. (*She reads.*) 'We saw Judith Bliss in a box at the Haymarket on Tuesday, looking as lovely as ever.' There now! I thought I looked hideous on Tuesday.

Sorel   You looked sweet. (*She goes to get herself some breakfast, and sits L. of* **Judith**.)

Clara *reappears, with a glass of orange-juice.*

Clara   There you are, dear. (*Placing it in front of* **Judith**.) Did you see that nice bit in the *Referee*?

Judith   *No* – the *Times*.

Clara   The *Referee*'s much better. (*She finds the place and hands it to* **Sorel**.)

Sorel (*reading*)   'I saw gay and colourful Judith Bliss at the Waifs and Strays Matinée last week. She was talking vivaciously to Producer Basil Dean. "'sooth," said I to myself, "where ignorance is Bliss, 'tis folly to be wise."'

Judith (*taking it from her*)   Dear *Referee*! It's so unselfconscious.

Clara   If you want any more coffee, ring for it. (*She goes out.*)

Sorel   I wish I were sitting on a lovely South Sea Island, with masses of palm-trees and coconuts and turtles—

Judith   It would be divine, wouldn't it?

Sorel   I wonder where everybody is.

Judith (*still reading*)   I wonder . . . Mary Saunders has got another failure.

Sorel   She must be used to it by now.

Simon *comes downstairs with a rush.*

Simon (*kissing* **Judith**)   Good morning, darling. Look! (*He shows her a newly-completed sketch.*)

Judith   Simon! How lovely! When did you do it?

Simon   This morning – I woke early.

Sorel   Let's see. (*Takes sketch from* **Simon**.)

Simon (*looking over her shoulder*)   I'm going to alter Helen's face; it's too pink.

Sorel (*laughing*)   It's exactly like her. (*Puts it on chair beside her.*)

Judith (*patting his cheek*)   What a clever son I have!

Simon   Now then, Mother! (*He gets himself breakfast.*)

Judith   It's too wonderful – when I think of you both in your perambulators.... Oh dear, it makes me cry! (*She sniffs.*)

Sorel   I don't believe you ever saw us in our perambulators.

Judith   I don't believe I did.

Simon, *having got his breakfast, sits at table R. of* **Judith**.

David *comes downstairs.*

David (*hilariously*)   It's finished!

Judith   What, dear?

David   *The Sinful Woman.* (*He kisses* **Judith**.)

Judith   How splendid! Read it to us now.

David (*takes chair from table and sits L.C.*)   I've got the last chapter here.

Judith   Go on, then.

Sandy *rushes in from the front door. On seeing everyone, he halts.*

Sandy Good morning. (*He bolts upstairs, two at a time.*)

There is a pause, they all look after him.

Judith I seem to know that boy's face.

David (*preparing to read*) Listen! You remember that bit when Violet was taken ill in Paris?

Judith Yes, dear. – Marmalade, Simon.

He passes it to her.

David Well, I'll go on from there.

Judith Do, dear.

David (*reading*) 'Paris in spring, with the Champs Elysées alive and dancing in the sunlight; lightly-dressed children like gay painted butterflies—'

Simon (*shouting to* **Sorel**) What's happened to the barometer?

Sorel (*sibilantly*) I don't know.

David Damn the barometer!

Judith Don't get cross, dear.

David Why can't you keep quiet, Simon, or go away.

Simon Sorry, Father.

David Well, don't interrupt again . . . (*Reading.*) '. . . gay painted butterflies; the streets were thronged with hurrying vehicles, the thin peek-peek of taxi-hooters—'

Sorel I love 'peek-peek'.

David (*ignoring her*) '– seemed to merge in with the other vivid noises, weaving a vast pattern of sound which was Paris—'

Judith What was Paris, dear?

David *Which* was Paris.

Judith What was Paris?

David   You can't say a vast pattern of sound *what* was Paris.

A slight pause.

Judith   Yes, but— What was Paris?

David   A vast pattern of sound *which was Paris*.

Judith   Oh, I see.

David   'Jane Sefton, in her scarlet Hispano, swept out of the Rue St Honoré into the Place de la Concorde—'

Judith   She couldn't have.

David   Why?

Judith   The Rue St Honoré doesn't lead into the Place de la Concorde.

David   Yes, it does.

Sorel   You're thinking of the Rue Boissy d'Anglais, Father.

David   I'm not thinking of anything of the sort.

Judith   David darling, don't be obstinate.

David (*hotly*)   Do you think I don't know Paris as well as you do?

Simon   Never mind. Father's probably right.

Sorel   He isn't right – he's wrong!

David   Go on with your food, Sorel.

Judith   Don't be testy, David; it's a sign of age.

David (*firmly*)   'Jane Sefton, in her scarlet Hispano, swept out of the Rue St Honoré into the Place de la Concorde—'

Judith   That sounds absolutely ridiculous! Why don't you alter it?

David   It isn't ridiculous; it's perfectly right.

Judith   Very well, then; get a map, and I'll show you.

Simon   We haven't got a map.

David (*putting his MS down*)   Now, look here, Judith –
here's the Rue Royale – (*He arranges the butter-dish and
marmalade pot.*) – here's the Crillon Hotel, and *here's* the Rue
St Honoré—

Judith   It isn't – it's the Boissy d'Anglais.

David   That runs parallel with the Rue de Rivoli.

Judith   You've got it all muddled.

David (*loudly – banging the table with his fist*)   I have *not* got
it all muddled.

Judith   Don't shout. You have.

Simon   Why not let Father get on with it?

Judith   It's so silly to get cross at criticism – it indicates a
small mind.

David   Small mind my foot!

Judith   That was very rude. I shall go to my room in a
minute.

David   I wish you would.

Judith (*outraged*)   David!

Sorel   Look here, Father, Mother's right. (*Starts to draw
map.*) Here's the Place de la Concorde—

Simon (*shouting at her*)   Oh, shut up, Sorel!

Sorel (*shouting back at him*)   Shut up yourself, you pompous
little beast!

Simon   You think you know such a lot about everything,
and you're as ignorant as a frog.

Sorel   Why a *frog*?

Judith   I give you my solemn promise, David, that you're
wrong.

David   I don't want your solemn promise, because I *know*

I'm right.

Simon It's no use arguing with Father, Mother.

Sorel Why isn't it any use arguing with Father?

Simon Because you're both so pig-headed!

David Are you content to sit here, Judith, and let your son insult me?

Judith He's your son as well as mine.

David I begin to doubt it.

Judith (*bursting into tears of rage*) David!

Simon (*consoling her*) Father, how can you!

David (*throwing his MS on floor*) I'll never attempt to read any of you anything again, as long as I live. You're not a bit interested in my work, and you don't give a damn whether I'm a success or a failure.

Judith You're dead certain to be a failure if you cram your books with inaccuracies.

David (*hammering the table with his fist*) *I am not inaccurate!*

Judith Yes (*Rising.*) you are; and you're foul-tempered and spoilt.

David Spoilt! I like that! Nobody here spoils me – you're the most insufferable family to live with—

Judith Well, why in Heaven's name don't you go and live somewhere else?

David There's gratitude!

Judith Gratitude for what, I'd like to know?

Sorel Mother, keep calm.

Judith Calm! I'm furious.

David What have you got to be furious about? Everyone rushing round adoring you and saying how wonderful you are—

Judith I am wonderful, Heaven knows, to have stood you for all these years!

Sorel Mother, do sit down and be quiet. (*Rises.*)

Simon (*rises and puts his arm round his mother*) How dare you speak to Mother like that!

During this scene, **Myra**, **Jackie**, **Richard** *and* **Sandy** *creep downstairs with their bags, unperceived by the family. They make for the front door.*

Judith (*wailing*) Oh, oh! To think that my daughter should turn against me!

David Don't be theatrical.

Judith I'm not theatrical – I'm wounded to the heart.

David Rubbish – rubbish – rubbish!

Judith Don't you say Rubbish to me!

David I *will* say Rubbish!

They all shout at each other as loud as possible.

Sorel		Sshhh, Father!
Simon		That's right! Be the dutiful daughter and encourage your father—
	(*together*)	
David		Listen to me, Judith—
Judith		Oh, this is dreadful – dreadful!

Sorel		The whole thing doesn't really matter in the least—
Simon		– to insult your mother—
David	(*together*)	The place de la Concorde—
Judith		I never realized how small you were, David. You're tiny.

The universal pandemonium is suddenly broken by the front door slamming. There is dead silence for a moment, then the noise of a car is heard. **Sorel** *runs and looks out of the window.*

Simon (*flops in his chair again*)   There now!

Sorel   They've all gone!

Judith (*sitting down*)   How very rude!

David (*also sitting down*)   People really do behave in the most extraordinary manner these days—

Judith   Come back and finish your breakfast, Sorel.

Sorel   All right. (*She sits down.*)

Pause.

Judith   Go on, David darling; I'm dying to hear the end—

David (*picks up his MS from the floor – reading*)   'Jane Sefton, in her scarlet Hispano, swept out of the Rue St Honoré into the Place de la Concorde—'

Curtain.